Contents

Introduction

I want to congratulate you for whatever the reason is that you purchased this book. In fact, I want to give you a gift. See, I have discovered that you retain more information by consuming it in various forms, so I would like to offer you a FREE audio download of this book at www.imnotcrazyimgrieving.com. I encourage you to LISTEN and READ the content included on these pages in order to maximize your learning and retention. (Or for those of you that just realized you can just listen and skip the reading all together, have at it ⏺) For the readers, let's continue.

You are NOT crazy, although grief can make you feel like you are losing your mind. The emotional, mental, and physical effects of grief can have you spinning. Sleepless nights, no appetite, zero focus or lapses in memory, body aches and pains, crazy emotional swings, and times of overwhelming sorrow can have you wondering if there is any hope for recovering from this.

Let me put your mind at ease. You will find solutions in this book. By the time we are finished, you will be able to say that you are now looking at your upcoming life season with much more optimism and hope.

What qualifies me to make such outlandish claims?

What is it that qualifies me to speak on this topic?

My qualifications are that I *have* no qualifications. This is great news for you, because that means, you do not need to be qualified either. It is possible to feel like you are screwing up for a long time, and also to know that you can still grab hold of these tools to heal, *today*.

What makes me an authority on how to navigate grief? I am not a licensed counselor, nor do I have a doctorate in Grief Therapy. The wisdom that I carry is an experiential wisdom. I earned my "degree" the hard way, through hand-to-hand combat with grief.

For you to glean any of the wisdom contained in these pages, you have to make a decision to listen to me. You are making the conscious choice to be open to the idea that my experience has taught me powerful healing techniques, and that I know what I am talking about, and have answers for you.

My experience with adversity and heartbreak started long before I experienced the death of a loved one.

Growing up in an alcoholic household where adultery, outbursts of anger, separations and reunification, and all the instability that those experiences bring, is what shaped my childhood.

I became accustomed to adversity.

I faced the adversity of dealing with sexual abuse at the age of 12, followed by keeping it a secret for two years before I ever told a soul. That led to one bad relationship after another. Because I held such little value for myself, I became an unwed young mother, finding out that I was pregnant with my son three days before my 19th birthday.

Marrying my son's father, believing marriage to be for the best, only led to more adversity and pain in the form of living with an addict who also struggled with anger issues. That ultimately led to a divorce, which led to more bad relationships, and more failed marriages.

My life was one trauma after another. Problem after problem seemed to have a compounding effect on my life. Failed relationships led to personal financial ruin and caused me to have to file for bankruptcy. This was shortly after being diagnosed with cancer at the age of 30. Two years later, having been diagnosed with another form of cancer, and continued relationship problems, should have made me an expert at adversity; instead I had become an expert at *living in* adversity. I had not yet become a master at *advancing through* adversity.

I have not shared this laundry list of problems to gain your sympathy, or to make you feel like I am any different from you. I share this list of trials so that you can see that I am just like you. That I have been through many challenges and adversities, and I failed at dealing with that for a very long time. Also, the realization that my inability to handle those things effectively only created more pain, trauma, and drama in my life.

This book is about the rest of the story.

This is the story of how I finally came to the end of that cycle. How, interestingly, it took even more significant life-shattering trauma and tragedy to learn the lessons that I am going to share with you in this book. I have paid an incredibly high price to acquire the information that is contained in these pages, and it is my hope and prayer that you will grab hold of every nugget of wisdom, every shared experience of heartache, and every hidden key on these pages.

It is my experience that we can live above any set of circumstances. That we can advance through adversity. We can use the adversity that life throws our way to put us in a better position in life. We can be strengthened and conditioned into wiser, stronger, and more empathetic versions of ourselves by harnessing the tools and resources that come with challenging times.

I know that this book holds the key to that power, for you to be set free from that which binds you. This book holds the keys for you to be able to live the life that you want to live, and I daresay live a life that you never even imagined possible.

This book is written in two main parts. The first part is going to be me sharing with you my experience of losing people that I love and walking through grief. I am going to share my story with you in rather a lot of detail, not for the sake of rehashing those details, or to magnify or glorify my own experience, but it is in those details that so many of the common traps and misconceptions around grief are hidden. These details will also help me to reveal to you so many of the treasures and gifts contained within grief.

I have also added these details for the sake of context, so that you will feel that you can relate to and resonate with me and what I have been through.

The second half of the book is dedicated to you, and to re-shaping your story. I am going to walk you through how to approach looking at this new season of life, so that you can take everything that has happened to you and put it into a framework that is going to lead you to places that you never imagined.

We are going to restore your hope. Together, we will map out a course to get you not only feeling that you are back to yourself, but also feeling better than you did before. You are going to learn some skills that are brand new to you, and most likely sharpen some skills that you already have.

This is your opportunity to grow and become a better version of yourself. A happier, more hopeful, empathetic, and caring individual that has something significant to contribute to the world. Living a life that you love. I know that may sound far-fetched right now. However, if you stick with me through this book, we will get there together.

Before you begin, take our Grief Assessment to know where you are starting from. You can take the assessment by going to www.griefassessment.com. We have also included this assessment in the back of the book for your reference.

If you are someone that likes to jump ahead to the instructional part of the book that pertains to you, I understand, I am built that way too. However, I encourage you to read my story anyway. It is important for you to read my story because you may see yourself in some capacity. It is important for you to experience being able to relate to the stories that I have shared for two reasons: The first reason is so that you know that you are not alone. You will likely see aspects of your own story in mine. The second reason is because it is crucial for you to begin to believe that it *is* possible to feel better. To start believing that you can heal, recover, and build the amazing life that I am promising you will have.

Are you ready? Let's begin.

Part 1:Sharing My Story

My Parents

My mother, Sharon, was born on December 7, 1954 in St. Paul, Minnesota. She was raised by two extremely Scandinavian parents. She met my father, Joseph, when they were both in high school. They were high school sweethearts and married shortly after she turned 18.

Soon after, she became pregnant and gave birth to my older sister Vicki. The troubles in their relationship were there from the beginning. My parents divorced shortly after having my sister, then remarried and had me, followed by my brother, Ryan.

My upbringing was in some ways normal, but in a lot of other ways, very abnormal and unhealthy. My mother built a home and a life with her husband and set about the task of raising her kids in the suburbs of Minnesota. My sister, brother, and I were very active in sports. All three of us played soccer. My father helped to coach, so we had a lot of activities and friendships through practice, games, and tournaments.

My father was a successful businessman, so we had a nice house with a pool. We were the first family on our block to get cable TV! From the outside, we looked like a typical suburban family. But on the inside, we dealt with the fallout of my father's alcoholism.

When I was in the third grade, my father left again, after my mother discovered that he had an affair with his secretary. He was gone for about nine months before they reunited again and continued in their marriage.

The Cycles of Addiction

One of the lasting effects of his alcoholic days was a car accident that he had when I was just three years old. He had passed out behind the wheel, and while unconscious, drove his car off the road. It flipped over several times before landing upside down.

That accident shattered the bottom four discs in his back and started a long list of medical complications and problems that he still struggles with to this day. Because of his ongoing back pain and discomfort, he was placed on pain medication.

Through the years, his dependency on these pills grew and grew. It created not only an incredibly high tolerance to pain pills, but also many other physical and psychological complications from being so dependent on the pills.

Vicki, Ryan, and I grew up through our father's constant cycles of substance and chemical dependence.

When I was in the fifth grade, he finally came to terms with the fact that he was an alcoholic and began seeking treatment. We went to treatment as a family and attempted to walk down the road of healing together.

Spain

When I was in sixth grade, we had an exchange student from Spain come and stay with us for a year. He decided to stay in Minnesota to attend college after he had completed his one-year stay.

We considered him part of our family, and we saw him regularly. When he and his family invited me to join him on his Christmas break trip home to Spain for a month, I jumped at the chance! Twelve-year-old me could not wait to explore the world, and experience Europe. After much discussion, my parents decided to let me go.

It was during that month-long trip to Spain that he sexually abused me (which is a story for an entirely different book). I came home and did not tell a soul for two years. I carried that secret before ultimately telling my parents about it when I was 14 years old.

Though my mother and I would talk about it again in my adult life, at the time, my parents did not handle it very well.

My father could not make eye contact with me for a while and after only two counseling sessions, we never really talked about it again. I moved forward and coped as best I could, which meant not well at all. My unstable and volatile homelife caused me to pursue attending college during my senior year in high school in order to get out of the house. I was the captain of our varsity soccer team and most likely gave up a full ride scholarship by making that choice, but I was desperate to get out of my home.

Unfortunately, the unresolved trauma of being abused at age 12 followed me to college and I struggled there. Although I earned a 3.4 GPA while working full time to support myself, the mental struggle of dealing with PTSD from the event took its toll. I came home before completing my freshman year.

At home my father continued to pull my mother through his cycle of addiction.

My plan to get out for good was to join the Air Force, God had other plans.

Meeting Q

This is the story of an unplanned, life-changing surprise that I was made aware of three days before my 19th birthday.

I will never forget going to the doctor's office that day. I was not at all thinking that I could be pregnant. I went to the doctor for what I thought was a urinary tract infection. Having noticed that I was a few days late for my period, I decided to ask them to run a pregnancy test. I sat in the waiting room, waiting for my results. Eventually the nurse called me back to talk to her.

To this day I do not understand why she did not take me into a room to tell me the news. She told me right there in the hallway that I needed to see a doctor, because my pregnancy test came back positive.

I must have looked like I was about to pass out because she instantly embraced me, propping me up, and then ushered me back down the hall and pushed me back into the waiting room. I stood there frozen for what felt like an eternity. The friend that had accompanied me to the doctor's office, sat across the waiting room and mouthed the words to me, "What is it?"

I stood there, in utter shock and disbelief, and announced to the entire waiting room, "I'm pregnant."

My friend quickly ran up and grabbed me and brought me to a seat.

10

I knew things would never be the same.

I later met with the doctor who informed me that my due date was mid-October and filled my hands with pamphlets about prenatal vitamins and all the things that I could expect in the months ahead.

The first call I had to make was to my unborn child's father. I was not excited to make that call, because he and I had broken up. We had not thought of it as a long-term relationship, because of my plan to leave in a few months to join the Air Force. I had come to the determination that it was not a relationship I was interested in keeping long-distance, so we broke up a few weeks before finding out about the pregnancy.

I called and asked him if he was sitting down. Then I informed him that we had a child on the way.

"No way!" was his response.

That was the beginning of the journey of life for Quintin Doyle Casey.

I am so thankful that the day I discovered I was pregnant, I immediately felt very connected to him as his mother. I loved him instantly. I felt protective over him. I am thankful that at my young age, and my unwed status, abortion never crossed my mind. I say that genuinely because I know that is not the case for a lot of people, and I consider it a gift from God that I never contemplated abortion or adoption. I knew instantly that I was going to have and love this child.

Quintin came into the world, October 21, 1997, six days after his due date. The longest six days of my life up to that point!

We began to do life together. In the long run, my original choice to break up with his father was the right choice, but at the time I was young, pregnant, and afraid of the future. So, he and I attempted to make our relationship work. Eight months into the pregnancy he proposed marriage, and I, out of fear, pregnancy hormones, or whatever, agreed.

I was young, naïve, and optimistic. I thought that if we got married, if we bought a house, if we did all the things that married couples are supposed to do, that somehow things would fix themselves.

After we got married and bought a house, the anger outbursts and the verbal abuse got worse instead of better. It started to escalate into physical altercations, smashing dishes, and punching holes in the wall.

I found out that he was stealing money from our joint account in order to support his drug habit. When I confronted him, it resulted in an explosive burst of anger.

All of this culminated in an early December morning when he had gotten up early with Quintin. I was upstairs lying in bed and I heard him yelling at Quintin because he was not eating his Cheerios. Then I heard a large *CRACK*. This was followed by Quintin screaming and crying. I ran downstairs. There was a red mark across Quintin's cheek.

That was it. I decided right then and there that I would end this marriage for the sake of my son and me.

We got divorced shortly thereafter.

About a year later, I met and married a man who would become Quintin's stepdad. His name was Shane. When Quintin was eight years old, he became a big brother to my beautiful daughter, Piper.

Throughout my marriage to Shane, I was in and out of the hospital due to my mental health struggles. The compounding effects of the abuse at 12, being raised in an unstable home, and an abusive first marriage took its toll. I was put on antidepressants, and that just made matters worse. I lost myself for three years. I couldn't tell where I stopped, and the meds started. What was me and what was the meds? I even attempted suicide on more than one occasion. All of this was too much for Shane to handle. He left when Piper was about six months old.

Not only was this devastating to me, but eight-year-old Quintin had now lost the only consistent father figure he had ever known.

A Challenging Season

Quintin's relationship with his biological father continued to be strained and toxic. Quintin could tell you at eight years old what marijuana smells like and could even identify a bong. Every time I sent him over to his father's house, I worried about what he was going to come back talking about. More times than I can count, he came back in tears and upset about something that had happened, or not happened, at his father's house.

Finally, after a rather severe altercation with his dad when Quintin was 12 years old, I informed Quintin's father that Quintin would no longer see him, except with the consent of a counselor.

Unfortunately, that was just enough to have his dad no longer really pursue a relationship or connection with him. From that point on, he stopped making time for Quintin. Quintin would see his dad occasionally at family outings and gatherings, but his father stopped having a significant presence in his life.

That hurt Quintin deeply. This coupled with the subsequent failure of my second marriage, and the stepfather who had been present in his life for several years leaving, left Quintin feeling abandoned, confused, hurt, and angry.

That is when his own anger started to show itself. At the age of 13, he started to seek solace and comfort from other places. Initially, it started with relatively normal behavior for a child his age. He was caught smoking cigarettes, staying out past curfew, and other somewhat harmless middle school antics.

I grew more and more concerned about his mental well-being, and honestly, about my ability to parent him and to cope with all that we were both facing.

Quintin, my mom and dad in Mexico

When Quintin was in eighth grade, he was caught with marijuana on the school bus. The school was threatening legal charges. It was at that point that I knew I needed to ask for help, so my sister Vicki and her husband Jeff graciously offered to let Quintin and I move into their home in order to get some support, direction, and more of a family structure to help raise Quintin. It also offered us the opportunity to change school districts and give him a fresh start and a new group of friends.

We uprooted our lives and moved in with them towards the end of his eighth-grade year. Only for him to end up gravitating to the same type of kids all over again.

Receiving Jesus

I need to add a very crucial detail here. I was not raised in a Christian home, so I did not grow up with faith. After failed relationships and struggling on my own, compounded by my first cancer diagnosis, I received the Lord as my Savior at age 30.

To this day, one of the greatest joys and honors of my life is that four years later, I was also able to lead my mother to the Lord. She had always known of God but did not really have a personal relationship with Him. After much discussion with me, and her observation of how I was changing, I was able to lead her in a prayer and help her to receive Jesus as her Lord and Savior.

Over the next five years, I witnessed my mother blossom right before my eyes. I saw my relationship with her, which had been contentious up until that point, change into a beautiful friendship. My mother became my best friend. We talked nearly every day on the phone. I watched her grow as a person and in her ability to be loving, patient, and kind.

I just loved that season of our lives.

My Father's Descent

We all were forced to deal with constant adversity as it relates to my father. There were years and years of chronic health issues. He was in and out of the hospital. He saw many doctors with many different opinions. At one point he was diagnosed with an auto-immune condition that attacked his nerve cells and caused severe pain in his hands, feet, and ankles, leading to eventual numbness. That diagnosis brought on a whole new slew of drugs and complications. His physical health continued to deteriorate, and his mental health was suffering. This would continue through the years.

For a very long time my experiences with my father existed in either one of two forms: Either he was wincing in pain, or he was completely drugged up and out of it. As a family, we all got used to this and prepared ourselves for his eventual decline and passing. When you see someone that you love struggling, and know that their health is declining, you lose a little bit of that person piece by piece as their health deteriorates. You brace yourself and prepare to lose them completely.

At this point, my mother and I were really believing and praying for healing and breakthroughs for my father. I cannot tell you how many nights I stayed awake, crying, fasting, praying, and inviting others to pray for my father's healing. With every hospitalization, with every new diagnosis, or new drug that doctors wanted to give him, I would just pray and cry out to God, believing in and affirming for his healing.

Seeing my father suffer so much was the heartache of my life at that point. I wanted more than anything, for him to be made well. My mother and I shared that desire.

But, on January 5, 2017, my sister texted me to let me know that my dad was - yet again - in the hospital because of a drug overdose and suicide attempt. Although a part of me was not surprised, something in me broke.

For whatever reason, that time, that hospitalization, that experience, was the final straw. I cried for three days. I thought for sure my father was going to die. I felt that my hopes for his healing would not be fulfilled, so I cried and grieved for my father.

He remained in the hospital and was immediately taken off every pain medication, which was incredibly dangerous because he had been on such high levels of medication for so long. They anticipated very severe withdrawal, but he had *no* withdrawal symptoms. None. I mean, he did not break a sweat, he did not vomit, nothing happened at all.

After five days, they released him, and I was convinced that this time there had been a breakthrough. That once and for all, my father was going to get off all the drugs. All the things that had been altering his mind and mood would be gone. He would be able to think clearly and see clearly for the first time in his adult life. My parents' marriage was going to be healed and made whole. Our family was going to be able to enjoy time together.

I was so excited! I was so confident that God was at work, and that He was doing a mighty thing in my father's life. A few days after he was released from the hospital, my father started to lose it. I do not know how to describe it except to say that he became agitated and disgusted at the entire medical system. He threw away every single medication he was prescribed. He flushed them all down the toilet. He said he would not take any medicine ever again, and that he was thinking clearly, for the first time.

I do think he had a new level of clarity of thought, but I do not think he had clarity of mind. He became very aggressive towards my mother which had previously been unusual for him. So much so, in fact, that they had a physical altercation, and he pushed her down. I remember my mother, calling me and emailing me because she did not know what to do. She was afraid for my father's life. She was afraid for his safety. She was afraid for her own safety.

She did not want to leave him, but she was afraid to stay. I implored her to reach out to the police, and to get some help. The police did show up, but they did not arrest him. They did let my parents know about some crisis resources and hotlines they could call if either of them thought about hurting themselves.

About a day later, my father *did* become concerned for his own safety and for the safety of my mother, so he called that crisis line and admitted himself back into the hospital.

He was back in the psych ward, initially through his own free will, but while he was there, they began to see that my father was deeply troubled. They put a psychiatric hold on him for his own protection. It went back and forth like that for a bit: the hospital would put a psychiatric hold on him, then he would stay there willingly, then the hospital would put him back on a hold when he threatened to leave. The doctors explored shock therapy, and all sorts of different therapies they wanted him to try. Mentally, he was not well.

It was during that time that my father decided that he was once again going to leave my mother. He had convinced himself that *she* was the problem and the source of all his pain. He confided this to me and asked me to keep it to myself. Or rather, he asked me not to tell my mother. I did not tell my mother, but I *did* tell my sister Vicki, who eventually *did* tell my mother.

When my mother found out that her husband of 40 years was planning to leave her after everything they had been through, things blew up even more. To make matters worse, he emptied out their joint bank account. He opened an individual bank account for himself after he took all the money out of their joint account. I do not know how he was even able to do that from inside a mental hospital, but clearly my father is determined when he wants to be.

The Loss

The hospitalization and all it entailed took up the entire month of January 2017. In and out of the hospital, on and off psychiatric hold. My father was erratic. He was convinced the hospital was violating his constitutional rights. He kept calling me asking me to look up statutes and specific constitutional laws because he planned to sue the entire hospital system when he got out.

His doctor filed a motion for him to be committed against his will. The way that works in the state of Minnesota is that the doctor makes a recommendation, and a social worker gets assigned to the case. The county social worker interviews the psychiatrist, the patient, and then one or two family members of the patient in order to assess the situation and the risks, and to determine what next steps should be taken. If the social worker deems that there is, in fact, significant risk, it will go to a judge and the judge will decide whether the commitment will be upheld or not.

If the social worker deems there is no risk, the social worker then has the authority to dismiss the case altogether. In our case, the social worker interviewed the psychiatrist, my father, and then spoke to both my mother and my sister about what was going on with him. My mother and sister explained to her that my father was not in his right mind that he was not acting in a sane way. They shared that he was saying threatening things and that all of us as a family were very afraid that if he left the hospital, he would hurt himself or others.

The social worker denied our request. We found out very abruptly on Saturday, January 28, that he was going to be released from the hospital.

Now with his plans to leave my mother, he had asked Ryan and I if he could come and stay with one of us until he could find a place to live on his own. I did not feel comfortable or safe at the idea of having him in my house. I knew that he was mentally unstable and that he was still a danger to himself. I could not, as a single mother, take that on. I also did not want to get caught in the middle of what was going on between him and my mother. I believed he was making a huge mistake. I felt he was doing tremendous damage by making the decision to leave her, and I was not going to support that. I explained to him that he could not come to my house. Ryan also felt that he did not want to be in the middle of this and explained to our father that he would not be able to find refuge in his house either. He would need to go to his own home and figure it all out with my mother.

However, my mother was petrified at the idea of him coming home. She was fairly convinced that he was still suicidal, and that he was just telling everyone what they wanted to hear so that he could be released from the hospital only to come home and finish the job. It was one of her biggest fears that he would kill himself in their home.

It was unsettling news for all of us. He went home, and I expected him to just pick up his clothes and leave since that is what he was telling all of us he was planning to do. But, to my surprise, he went home and stayed. Saturday. Sunday. Monday. I spoke to my mother every day to check on her and to make sure that they were both okay. When I spoke to her on Tuesday, January 31, I was surprised to find that he was still there.

I said, "Mom, Dad's there? I thought he was leaving! What is he doing still there?"

Her response was, "Well, we're just taking it day by day. You know, things are rough, but we're trying to work on it."

I replied, "Mom, what are we going to do to help you? What are we going to do to get you support? This is a stressful time and a scary place for you to be. How can we support you? Are you going to go to a counselor or a Christian women's group?"

She said, "Yeah. I think I would like to check out a Christian women's group."

After this decision was made, we chatted a little bit more. I had a date scheduled that night and my mother and I were both excited about it.

She said to me, "You'll have to call me tomorrow and let me know how it goes." The call ended, I went about my day and I went on my date that night.

The next morning, I was awakened by a call at about six in the morning from my father. He was weeping.

He said that he found my mother passed away, next to a bottle of pills.

Chaos and Pain

Now, if you were led to read this book, it is likely that you can relate to the feeling of utter shock and helplessness that I felt in that moment.

I just remember yelling back through the phone, "No, no, no, Dad!"

"Yes, Kelli, yes," he repeated. "It's true.

I said, "I'm coming over," and hung up the phone.

My brain did not work. I tried to go into my closet to get sweatpants and boots. After all, it was February 1 in Minnesota. I tried getting dressed. I literally could not put pants on. I could not put shoes on.

The phone rang again. It was my dad again saying that I could not come over because the police were still there. They were still dealing with the crime scene and they would not let anyone else in the house.

I could not accept that. "No!" I cried into the phone.

He put a police officer on the phone. The officer explained that I would not be let in the house until they were done with the crime scene and their procedures were complete. I asked him to please call me back as soon as they were done so that I could go over. He assured me he would. After I hung up, I just sat and cried. I called a pastor friend, sobbing. I was in pain. Shock. Totally numb.

About 45 minutes after we first spoke, the police officer finally called back and told me that I could now go to the house. I will never forget the drive over for as long as I live. Though my parents' house was only 15 minutes away, that morning it took me an eternity. I was in a shocked haze, and I kept turning down the wrong streets.

As I finally pulled up to the house, the last police officer was just leaving. I do not remember the details of our conversation. I remember him saying that he was sorry for my loss and that they had found a bunch of pills next to her body, also that it would be a while until they knew conclusively from an autopsy what really happened.

I went in the house and walked into the room where my mother had passed just hours before. I saw the bed with blood and urine on the sheets. I stayed in that room probably longer than I should have, letting the scene burn into my heart, soul, and mind.

I walked into the living room where my dad was hunched over in his chair. I tried talking to him, but he just kept repeating, "I'm sorry."

Ryan arrived shortly after that. Ryan and I sat in awkward, stunned silence as our father said repeatedly that he was sorry. Then he suddenly said, "I waited too long. I should have called when she was still talking."

After a while, he started to give us his account of what happened.

He told us that two days prior, he and my mother had an argument. The following day, she had written him a letter that referred to that argument. Later that day, she told him she was not feeling well, and went to bed. She did not go to their bedroom, but to the back bedroom of their two-bedroom house.

Though he knew she was upset, he said that he felt he had no reason to be concerned about her. If they had disagreements, it was not unusual that they would sleep in separate bedrooms.

We know that she had locked the door because when we arrived on the scene, the door handle had been removed. It struck me as odd that my father was stating that he had not been concerned, when apparently he felt concerned enough to remove the door handle in order to gain access to the room.

"Why did you take the handle off if you weren't concerned for her?" I asked him.

He responded, "What would happen if there was a fire? How would she get out?"

I had difficulty even typing these words, they are so preposterous. My parents lived in a small house and the room in question has two large windows. My mother would have no trouble escaping if there was a fire or other disaster.

His story was that though he was not concerned for her safety, he went to check on her several times throughout the night. He claims that he would go and check on her, lying next to her in bed. He said that he checked her vital signs throughout the night, yet also repeated that he felt no cause for concern.

He said that did not think she had done anything to harm herself.

He cited three specific times that he checked on her and found that she was breathing and had a pulse. At around midnight, then again at 2 am., and then again at 3 a.m.

He went to check on her one last time around 5 a.m. That is, he said when he noticed that she had blood coming out of her nose, she had urinated herself, and he saw the bottle of pills next to her. That is when he called 911.

By the time the ambulance and the police arrived she was already gone.

That is the story that my father told us the morning of February 1, 2017. In that moment, on that day, my life as I knew it was shattered.

In the weeks that followed, as I recalled what he had shared that day, I began to question everything I had ever known to be true about my father, my family, and my upbringing. One of the things he had also shared with us that day was that the car accident from way back when I was three years old was not a result of him passing out behind the wheel, but in fact had been a suicide attempt. He intentionally drove that car off the side of the road, in an attempt to kill himself.

Everything that I had been told my whole life and any understanding that I had of my family was completely destroyed.

I had so many questions about the events of that night. However, the police were assuming that my mother's death was a suicide. Vicki and I expressed our concerns to the police about the fact that this was not a clear-cut suicide.

When I called the police myself and asked what my father had shared with them, I was told that they could not share a lot of details, but that my father had said he and my mother had been arguing, and that she went to bed and that my father did not feel that he had any cause for concern. Then he found her in the morning, passed away.

I wanted to make sure the detective knew everything. "Did he tell you that he just got released from the psych ward?" I asked.

"No, he didn't tell me that," the detective responded.

I asked, "Did he tell you that he had a physical altercation with my mom a few weeks ago that landed him in the psych ward in the first place?"

"No, he didn't tell me that," the detective responded once again.

I said, "Well, you may want to consider some of those things before you rule it as a suicide. Did he tell you that he emptied their bank account?"

"No, he didn't tell me that," the detective responded a third time.

Vicki had a similar conversation with another detective and in spite of these conversations the police still concluded that my mother died by suicide. They cited two main reasons that led them to that conclusion; the strongest reason they had was that my father spoke to two separate officers the morning of my mother's passing and because his story was consistent both times, they felt that was an indication that my father was telling the truth. The second reason was that the autopsy revealed that there were no signs of struggle or force on her body. Those two pieces of evidence were enough for them to decide that it was a suicide. Therefore, there was nothing more for them to investigate.

I now saw my father for the first time as someone who was very dangerous and dishonest.

Bamboozled?

The most hurtful part for me at that time was that I felt bamboozled by God. Here I was, so convinced that God was going to save my father. I had cried out to God and surrendered my father fully to the Lord just weeks before , praying, "God, I release him completely to you, to have your way in his life, to do whatever you need to do to reveal yourself to him and to heal him. I can't carry it anymore. I give it completely to you, God."

Then all this happens.

I felt so betrayed. I felt like my entire faith was a joke, some cruel joke that the universe had played on me. A devastating lie that I had believed in, that all this hope that I had been taught was just make-believe.

At the time, I was working in a leadership role in a ministry, and I felt completely ill-equipped for the role. I did not want anything to do with God, ministry, or leadership. I was very hurt and felt deeply betrayed.

As the months passed, my father's story changed several times. New pieces of information entered the story nearly every day. He had contended the whole time that he was still planning to leave her, but that he had not yet told her. A couple of months later, he reversed this story and said that he did tell her he was planning to leave. On top of it, within a few months of my mother's passing, my father began dating a new woman.

I was infuriated and enraged that the system had failed us so miserably. I was so angry at the police department, for not so much as even asking questions, and for not digging beneath the surface for the truth. I was angry at the hospital system, and the social worker who allowed my father to leave the hospital against everyone's recommendations. To this day, l feel that the hospital system played a significant part in her passing.

My dad should never have been released.

I sat swimming in this pool of questions, anger, confusion and frustration. I decided God was not the place in which I would find help. I was so angry at Him. I could not go to church at first, and I remember the first time I returned to church; all these people were singing about a faithful God and I wanted to punch them all.

The anger that rose up in me that day was almost uncontrollable. I wanted to yell at them, "You are all so stupid! You've been fooled!"

Thankfully, one of my friends worked at the church and was watching me, and she could see on my face that I needed to get out of there. She led me to her office, and I collapsed on the ground, weeping and sobbing.

I was not really on speaking terms with God. When I did finally talk to Him, I let Him know that it was going to be a one-sided conversation. I was not interested in what He had to say, and I informed him that He was going to listen to a few things that I had on my mind.

I informed Him that I would no longer be tithing. At least for a year. I figured that I had had a year's worth of pain and suffering, so a year of keeping the tithe for myself for damages caused was more than fair. He owed me at least that!

I was searching for answers and demanding justice. I was keeping in touch with my father so that, poking and prodding through our conversations, I could get the truth from him.

I called the examiner's office to check on the toxicology report that seemed to be taking forever. It was supposed to take six weeks for the report, but months had passed. Every time I called I would get the runaround. When I finally did speak with the medical examiner directly, she said that they were still waiting for the results.

She said that the reason there was a hang up was that the bottle of medication that was found next to my mother's body was *not* the drug that she overdosed on. The bottle next to her was Vicodin, and there was zero Vicodin in her system. They thought that was rather confusing. Further, it turned out that the drug that killed her was not a prescription that was hers.

I asked quickly, "Was it Dilaudid? Was it Dilaudid that she died from?"

The examiner said, "How did you know that?"

I said, "That's one of the many medications that my father's on." The one that he supposedly overdosed on earlier that month.

She said, "Well, that clears it up. Yes, it was Dilaudid."

Once they were able to release the medical report, the police closed their case. Even though the medication that killed her was not the medication found next to her.

The conclusion was that she had taken her life.

Piper, me, Quintin, and his girlfriend Ashley at my mom's funeral.

God Answers

All I can remember from that time about my day to day life was that I was a ball of emotion. I remember the heaviness and the sorrow feeling so intense and so real that I literally thought it would swallow me whole. I could not think straight. I could not sleep.

Nights were the worst. My appetite was gone, my focus was gone. Everything was a mess. I realized that I also did not have the capacity to do the job that I was working at the time. Thankfully I worked for a gracious man who understood my situation and helped me to find a similar position in another organization with far less responsibility. A place where I could just kind of show up to work, and go through the motions, and have time to heal.

For several months after her passing, that is exactly what I did. I just went through the motions, I would pick up the phone several times a day to call her, only to remember I could not call her anymore.

I finally did cry out to God. I started demanding answers from Him.

Where was He? How could He let this happen? How could this do any good?

I did not understand it.

I decided to go back to church again, but I still had no intention of paying the tithe, as I had previously informed Him. When I went to church that day something sparked inside of me prompting me to tithe. I grumbled to God and begrudgingly said, "Okay, God, I'm going to tithe. I don't want to, but I'm going to. This is me coming towards you a little bit, God.".

I walked down to the front and dropped my tithe in the bucket. I knelt down at the altar. I felt the Lord say to me, "You have never been more beautiful than you are in this moment." I wept.

I cannot say that God healed my heart or answered all my questions in that moment. What I did find in my deepest, darkest place, in my place of anguish, and anger and confusion and frustration, was God. And I found him to be exactly the same as He always was. His gentle, loving, welcoming response was the God that I had always known and I knew in that moment a foundational true faith,was born in me. I knew that God is the same yesterday, today, and tomorrow and that no matter what circumstances come your way, you can always find Him, and you will always find Him the same.

That was the beginning of my journey of healing

I wish I could say that He waved a magic wand and made everything better, but He did not. I still had a lot of questions. I still had a lot of anger. I still wanted justice. I wanted to take on my father, the police department, the hospital, the county. I wanted to call media outlets. I was demanding justice and the hurt, the pain, was still so strong as time went on.

I began to feel more and more isolated in my pain. Because of the traumatic and tragic circumstances surrounding my mother's death, and especially because of all the suspicion and questions with my father, it felt surreal, like, *this can't be my life*. The joke that my friends and I had was that my life was like an episode of *Dateline*.

I could not believe that this was happening to me. My mother was gone and my father might have had a hand in it; he was not telling the truth and nobody seemed to care. The more that time went on, the more everyone else moved on with their lives. Yet, I just couldn't. The fact that they were moving on was offensive to me. How dare they go on with their lives? My mother is gone. My best friend is gone. The person who loved me unconditionally and had my back and wanted to know every detail about my life, was gone.

She was gone from this planet and nobody seemed to care.

Or if they did care, people just did not know what to do. They did not know what to say. They did not know how to comfort me. Because of that, many of them chose to say nothing, which hurt even more because I felt like I was the sad friend that nobody wanted to be around. I felt very alone in my pain. I felt like nobody understood. I felt like nobody could help me make it better. I went to a suicide support group, and I did find some temporary comfort, being in a room full of people who were going through the same thing.

The part that scared me out of my mind was that there were people in that group who were several years out from losing someone they loved to suicide and were still expressing the same amount of struggle that I was experiencing. Several people in that group were unable to work. Many of them reported that they were barely functioning. They shared that every day was such a struggle. Every day was a challenge. Every day, there were triggers. Every day, they were just barely getting by.

While I was encouraged and comforted to find people who understood what I was facing, I was terrified that this was now destined to be my lot in life. That for the rest of my life I would just be enduring. That I would just be trying to get by. I would move from one painful encounter to another, and one triggering memory to another, one empty holiday to another.

That sounded awful to me.

I sort of settled into this, this, "going through the motions" existence. I was a mother with two children. I had a job and bills to pay. I had to keep moving as best I could, but inside I was full of sorrow, despair, and hopelessness.

Starting My Journey

I lived like this for several months, until I went to a leadership conference that I was required to attend through my job.

I remember wondering how I would have the presence of mind to even hear what the speakers were saying. It was still incredibly difficult for me to concentrate, and the idea of sitting still for several hours, listening to speakers, was not something that I was looking forward to.

But then I heard one of the speakers at this conference named Immaculee Ilibagiza, who shared her story with us of surviving the Rwandan genocide. She shared in horrific detail about how she lived for 90 days in a bathroom with eight other women, terrified every day as soldiers came to sweep the area to eradicate her people. She shared how she heard over the radio literally a million people being massacred around her. She listened over the radio while her entire family and the complete village next door, was totally wiped out.

Immaculee shared about eventually coming out of the bathroom, and the journey of healing. She revealed how God walked her through a journey of forgiveness, restoration, and peace, to the point that she was able to go meet the man that killed her family in prison and forgive him. But the most important part for me about everything she said was the way that she shared it. I saw this woman standing on stage, who was whole and happy, who had joy and peace. She now lives in New York and has two children, and she is sharing her story to make a difference in the world. But even more significant than the difference she is making in the world was the peace that I saw resting on her. I saw that she genuinely was happy; she had been healed.

At that moment, a light bulb went on.

This was the first person in the six months since my mother's passing that I met or saw that had been through something worse than what I was facing, and the idea rose up in me: that if she could do it, then I can do it. Whatever God did for her, He would do for me.

Me and Immaculee

A little seed of hope was planted in me that day. I began to have hope that I could get better and I began to believe that one day I could, in fact, be happy again.

That began my journey of discovering what it was going to take for me to walk through to a place of healing.

I pressed into the Lord and started reading in the Word and reading about grief. I began to revisit the concept that God is good, and trusting that He does, in fact, have plans to prosper me even though at the time I could not yet see it or understand it. I began to operate emotionally from a place that superseded my understanding.

Next, I started to pay attention to how my body was feeling. I paid attention to the things that helped me feel better, and the things that that caused me to feel stuck. I paid attention to the times when I felt sad and wanted to sit with the sadness, and I started to put a limit on how long I would entertain those feelings or cry. I would find ways to start moving my body and my mind again, I started to see my thinking ability come back and I got more engaged and took on more work projects. I started to come out of my shell and get back to living life.

My mom

My Message to My Mother

God really ministered to me during that time, as I was crying out to Him and asking, "Where were You, in all of this? How could You let this happen? How could You let me be so blindsided? Why didn't You protect me? Why didn't you protect her?"

He reminded me that a couple months before all this happened, He had encouraged me to write cards to the people that I loved in order to bless them. To take the time to write down what they mean to me, and to send it to them in the mail. Being Scandinavian, we are not always known for our grand gestures of emotion or affection. So, this would be out of the ordinary for my family for sure. I, thankfully, followed His prompting and sent a card to exactly three people, letting them know what they meant to me. My mother was one of the three.

I sent the card in November of 2016, just a few months before her passing. In it, I wrote how blessed I was to be her daughter. I let her know that the impact she was making in our family was going to be felt through me, my children, and their children's lives, for years to come.

When the Lord reminded me about that card that I had written, I went back to my parent's house and I found that my mother had kept the card close to her. She kept it in her nightstand drawer, and it was clearly meaningful to her although she never mentioned it to me. She never once mentioned that she received it. She never brought it up, but she kept it and when I reread the card, I could not believe what I had written. I had basically said everything I would have wanted to say to my mom, if I had known she was about to pass away.

Here is what I wrote on the card:

Mom —

I don't tell you enough how lucky I am to have you as my mom. Watching you love Dad and stand by his side is an inspiration. Not only that, but the way you are always looking for things to keep us together and do nice things for us. You are teaching me to be a better woman. Your influence will live on in me and my kids and their families for many years to come. Thank you! Love you!

Kelli

The Lord really showed me that He was providing for me in that moment through His prompting me to write that card. A few months before she passed away, He made a way for me to be able to say to my mother everything that I carried in my heart.

My Mother's Message to Me

Just as I got to tell her what was in my heart, my mother got to do the same thing. I mentioned earlier in this book that I had been sexually abused when I was 12. In the December before she passed, my mother asked if she could take me out to lunch. As we seated, she started crying.

"What's wrong?" I asked her.

She said, "Kelli, my biggest regret in life is that I let you go to Spain. I hold myself responsible for what happened to you."

I said, "Mom, what are you talking about? Of course, you're not responsible."

She recalled that apparently right before I was set to leave for Spain, I got cold feet, and did not want to go. She and my father got in a big fight about it. My father was siding with me, saying if I did not want to go, they should not force me. But my mother felt strongly that I should go. They had already bought the plane ticket, and she felt that I was just nervous because I was young. She thought that I would really regret it if I did not go. She was sure that I would get over there and have an amazing time, an adventure that I would cherish for my entire life. She was adamant that I go.

When she shared this with me, I didn't even remember having feelings of not wanting to go. But from what my mother said, apparently, I did, and she was the one who insisted that I go. At the time she shared this with me, it was 27 years after the fact. So, she had been walking around with this regret and shame for 27 years. She was finally able to confide in me over lunch that day, and I was able to completely forgive her and let her know that she did not need to carry the responsibility for that.

Even though her death was sudden and tragic, we were both able to have the conversations we needed to have with each other before she died. I was able to say what I wanted to say, and she was able to confide in me her biggest regret, and to hear directly from my mouth, that I did not blame her. I forgave her. I do not hold it against her.

I am so thankful for that gift.

A Season of Healing

Those two incidents became the string that helped me stay connected to God, and to begin to dare to believe that He was doing something bigger than I could understand. Even though in the moment it seemed so confusing, and so contrary to who I knew Him to be, and I was so blinded by the pain. He showed me through those two circumstances of emotional communication with my mother that He was looking out for us. He showed me that through all of it He was at work, leading and guiding me, and I began to trust that if He was leading me then, that he was still leading me, even now.

This is one of the opportunities you have, to go looking for the places where God showed up in your story. I can guarantee that if you look back at some of the details of your story, you will see that God's faithfulness is there. I know that there are things He was saying to you, many ways that He was speaking to you, providing for you, protecting you, instructing you. Things that maybe you cannot recognize right now, or you did not recognize in the moment when it happened. But I want to invite you, as you continue to read this book and as you continue to learn about the steps and the framework for healing, to go back for yourself and dissect what happened and look for your own little note cards or meaningful conversations.

Quintin's Path

Quintin's entire high school experience was one wrapped in turmoil. I saw him slipping further and further away from me. He started getting caught with different kinds of drugs. What began as cigarettes became occasional marijuana use, then turned into regular marijuana use, then turned into experimenting with and using other kinds of drugs. For example, Aderol, among other things, which to my horror I found were readily available in high school.

I started to get an understanding of the significance of the problem in his junior year of high school… when my father discovered that a bottle of painkillers was missing from his home. We realized that Quintin was the only one that had access and opportunity to take them.

Now the resourceful mother that I am, I had spent time researching high and low the different options for recovery and rehabilitation. Being a single mother who worked in the non-profit world, there were not many options that I could afford. Even with insurance, the co-pay alone for a short-term program at the local rehabilitation facility would cost $8,000. Not only that, but all the facilities were free will facilities, so until or unless Quintin admitted that he had a problem and *wanted* to seek help, there was nothing I could do as a parent to send him somewhere that would require him to stay there and get help.

We held a family intervention and told him that he needed to get help. My parents, sister, and brother-in-law were all part of it. We sat with Quintin and told him what we were seeing happening to him and shared the concern that we had. We wanted him to get help.

We explained to him that if he refused to get help, things like his car and ability to go hang out with friends or to keep his job would all be at risk. He reluctantly agreed to go to a day-treatment program, where he did get sober for a short period of time.

While I was encouraged to see Quintin sober, it was difficult and disheartening to see the level of sadness that rose to the surface when he stopped numbing the pain with drugs. Intense sadness and sorrow. He had a tough time dealing with that, to the point that he had suicidal ideation.

He just could not cope with all the feelings that were coming out, so he relapsed quickly. At that point I told him I knew he needed more help, he needed to go to a living facility for a long period of time to get the help, support, and tools needed in order to live a healthy, happy, sober life. I let him know that he would need to make that choice to go to a long term, live-in treatment facility or he that he would not be allowed to stay at my house anymore.

I thank God for the grace that I knew at the time that that is absolutely what I needed to do. That was the stance that I needed to take for his life and well-being.

Despite my intentions to help him recover, he came home one day soon after that, high on marijuana and Xanax, and informed me that he would not be going to treatment, and he would be leaving. That was the first time I saw him severely impaired. He could hardly keep his eyes open and was not able to keep up his side of the conversation. It was the first time I thought I was losing my son. So, he spent the summer of his junior year going into senior year, not living at home, couch-hopping from one place to the next, doing God knows what. I would get a call every now and then from the police to let me know that they had picked him up after curfew, or they had caught him with some marijuana.

Every time he and his friends were caught doing something, they would just slap his wrist and let them all go.

I could not get anybody else or do anything else to help me help him.

Then he got caught shoplifting a small item from a home goods store, and the police called me again. This time, he was going to have a court date. I called the court to ask if I could speak to the judge, if I could let them know that my kid had a problem. To share that he did not need jail, he needed help.

I wanted the judge to know that this drug issue had gone on and on, and it was getting worse instead of better. I desperately needed the system or someone to stand up and help me get him the help he needed. I was informed that because he was 17, he had the right to confidentiality. Though because he was not yet 18, I was still legally responsible for him and was required to come to the court date. I was not able to reach the judge, but I did speak to someone that told me that I could write a letter to the judge, but there was no guarantee that the judge would read it or consider it. So, I wrote the letter explaining to the judge everything we had been through and asked for his help to get my son some help.

Thankfully, the judge *did* read my letter, and did not mandate him to jail, but rather mandated him to get some treatment. It was not inpatient treatment; he had to complete an outpatient program and attend counseling sessions. He was also put on probation where he would have random drug testing for the next year.

Quintin realized that his way of doing things was not working out so well for him.

He asked me if he could move back home. I agreed but had very structured expectations and obligations in place. He knew that I could drug test him at any time and he knew that he was expected to go to school and work.

His senior year of high school was a very sweet time for us. He started dating a young lady named Ashley, who was a good influence on his life. She became a part of our household and family. Quintin reconnected with his faith and introduced Ashley to church and faith as well.

Quintin did very well in school that year. He went to an alternative school, and easily caught up on his missed credits. He ended up graduating early and getting awesome grades his senior year. He kept a job, got baptized at church, and maintained a relationship with Ashley.

I remember going to his high school graduation and being so thankful! There was a time when I didn't know that he would make it to 18 alive, much less graduate high school, so we celebrated. I was even more surprised to find out that he wanted to go to college, and that he had applied to and got admitted at a nearby college, about an hour and a half away from home.

Quintin and I at his graduation, June 2016.

Part of me was concerned that the freedom that college brings would be a dangerous thing for him. That while he had been able to have success this past year, I knew that it was under a very structured environment where Ashley and I were with him virtually all the time. We kept an eye on all that he did, and I knew the freedom that dorms would bring. Nevertheless, as many parents find, you get to a point where you have to let your kids go to explore, discover, and learn on their own. I had been so encouraged by all the positive steps I had seen him take the year before that I was thrilled that he was wanting to better his future and go to college.

So, I drove him down to his college so he could begin his journey.

Quintin and his best friend Michael the day they moved into the dorms.

He had only been there about a month when he got a ticket for minor consumption.

Perhaps you would think that this incident would have sparked all kinds of alarms in me, and fears that he was going down a destructive path, but I was encouraged. Not because he got a ticket for consumption, but because he called and *told* me. He did not try to hide it, he did not try to deny it, he was disappointed in himself and called and shared with Ashley and I what had happened.

We discussed how he was going to make adjustments and corrections in order to avoid future slips. I encouraged him to seek Christian support on campus, and to find other students that shared his faith, so that he could have a community of support.

Unfortunately, I do not think that he ever did.

He continued to struggle to find his place in college. The classes were a lot harder than he had anticipated. Balancing work, school, and all the freedom was not easy for him. He was really struggling when he came home for Christmas break. He was considering not going back and was having a tough time finding his place. Ultimately, he did decide to go back and at least give the college experience a complete year before deciding if it was the right fit for him.

It was shortly after he returned to school that my mother took her life.

I will never forget having to call him and let him know what had happened. I just remember him saying, "No, no, no!" Just as I had.

He could not believe how she died. It shattered his world and broke his heart. I found out later that Quintin went on a bender after this, doing every kind of drug that he could get his hands on. I believe he stopped going to class after that. He seemed to withdraw altogether.

None of this was made known to me at the time until it escalated to the point that Quintin himself threatened suicide. He and Ashley had been on-again/ off-again, because of the distance. He had mistakenly started a relationship with a girl while trying to restore his relationship with Ashley. Both girls found out, and the jig was up.

It was then that he told Ashley of his intentions to end it all. He sent her a picture from on top of a bridge. I got a call from Ashley letting me know that Quintin had attempted suicide. That same shock and grief I felt when I lost my mother took the breath out of my lungs. Once we were able to get more details, we found out that he was hanging out at a bridge and making threats.

Luckily, Ashley remembered a spot where he had taken her on a campus visit that had a bridge. She called the police and described him and his car and let them know where that location was. The police went and found him there. We were notified that he was at an area hospital, and we could come down and get him.

Quintin, Piper and I on the very bridge where he threatened to take his life.

Vicki, Ashley, and I made the hour and a half drive down to the hospital to find out what was going on. By the time we got there he was agitated and dismissive, insisting that the whole thing was just a misunderstanding. He was irritated more than anything. When I spoke with the social worker at the hospital and explained the history and the concern because of my mother's recent passing, she explained that they did not have any psych beds open for him, and that if we felt that he needed to be placed in a psychiatric ward, he would need to wait for up to three weeks, and would likely be placed in a hospital far away. When I explained the pattern of drug abuse and addiction, she literally told me she had no help for that. That is something I would have to explore on my own. (It is a travesty if this is the state of our medical systems. If we can't find help from social and mental health care workers, how are we going to overcome this epidemic?)

We brought Quintin home and all shared our concerns with him. I told him at that point that he could go to rehab, join the military, or join the school of ministry that was offered by our church, and if he would pursue any one of those three options I would move heaven and earth to help him. But if he was not interested in pursuing any one of those three things, I could not help him. He would not be allowed to live with me, and he would have to figure out his choices for himself.

He went back to school and continued the same behavior as before.

Classes ended for the summer so when everyone else went back home, Quintin spent yet another summer homeless. For a few nights, he slept in a park, then he stayed with a cousin for a few weeks until drug use and arguments in the household got him kicked out. He ended up getting a job at a nearby golf course and was literally living at the golf course for a few weeks.

The golf course ended up closing, so he was out of options. It was a tough time.

He ended up back on my doorstep pleading for a place to stay and requesting help.

I let him stay with the condition that he could stay for three weeks in order to come up with a plan. I informed him if he was going to stay, he had to be drug free, he had to go to a doctor, and do whatever the doctor recommended.

I took him to the doctor, and to my horror realized how much he had wasted away. My 6'1" kid was 132 pounds. His eyes were sunken, and he was so depressed, and helpless. The doctor sent him to a psychologist, and a psychiatrist who recommended an anti-anxiety medication and an antidepressant medication. I told him if he was going to stay with me, he needed to be looking for a job, so eventually he got a job at a nearby gas station. He started taking the medication, getting solid sleep, eating multiple times a day, and he gained eight pounds in a couple of weeks.

Before we knew it, the three weeks came and went. It was the time that he was supposed to leave according to our agreement, but he was not ready to go. After a couple more weeks of me witnessing his decline and realizing that he was not keeping our agreement, I had to kick him out again. This time he had nowhere to go, and I almost ended up bringing him to the homeless shelter I was working for at the time. Ultimately, he asked me to drop him off at a "friend's" house, which I reluctantly did. My heart sank as I drove away, not knowing where he would end up or if he would be OK.

Eventually Quintin ended up making his way back down to his college town Mankato, moving in with roommates, and finding employment in town.

My New Season

It was right around this time that I received a job offer with an opportunity to move to Florida. After much prayer and consideration, I felt confident that the Lord opened this door in Florida, and that for my daughter Piper and I, it was a chance at a new beginning and a fresh start.

The move to Florida was completely orchestrated by God. Growing up in Minnesota, I had always hated the winters. I would brace for them every year and endure them year after year. For as long as I can remember, I have always dreamed about moving somewhere warm, and escaping the winters. But then life happens, you have kids, and you find yourself tied to your circumstances. The fact that Quintin and my daughter Piper had different fathers meant that me moving out of state would require the support and approval of multiple people. So I had resigned myself to stay in Minnesota, at least until Quintin graduated high school. After that I would be able to explore the idea of moving elsewhere.

It was in the middle of January of 2018, (the dead of winter, the coldest part of the year) that Piper's father, Shane, asked if I would consider moving down to Naples, Florida. His parents had a place down there, so they had been vacationing there for years.

My understanding of Naples was that it was filled with rich old people. I did not have an interest in living there.

At the time I was working for a homeless shelter and addiction recovery organization in the Twin Cities called Union Gospel Mission, and I had grown to love my work. I had been working in faith-based nonprofit organizations for nearly 10 years. In order to appease Shane and to dismiss the idea of moving to Florida, I told him that I would look online to see if there were any homeless shelters or addiction recovery centers in Naples.

To my total surprise, when I looked online, I discovered a large organization in the heart of Naples that was a homeless shelter and addiction recovery facility called St. Matthew's House. It was not only located right in Naples but was doing wonderfully innovative and amazing work in the area of homelessness and addiction recovery. The day I looked them up, they had just posted an open position the day before.

The one problem was the position that they posted was two steps above the position that I held at the time. Plus, I did not meet any of the qualifications they were requiring in terms of education, or length of leadership. But, if I had learned anything about God in the 10 years of walking with Him, I knew that He could open any door and close any door according to His will. I wrote a cover letter and applied.

Even after I applied, I told God, "Florida is nice and all, but I am not going unless you're in it."

I called my sister that week and mentioned to her that I had applied for the job in Florida. My whole family had lived their entire lives in Minnesota. None of us had ever lived outside of the state, except for a family cabin in Wisconsin. Any Minnesotan will tell you that Wisconsin is an extension of Minnesota. None of us had left the state to go to college, nobody had taken a job outside of the state. We were all born, raised, and living in Minnesota.

So, when I called my sister and mentioned to her that I had applied for a job down in Florida, her response was, "I guess we're *all* moving to Florida!"

That was the confirmation I needed. It turns out her husband's company was going to have a general manager position opening in Florida, and he intended to apply. The fact that my sister and brother in law, who like me had lived their whole adult lives in Minnesota, were also considering a move to Florida was confirmation to me that God was up to something.

I was surprised to hear back from St. Matthew's human resources department shortly after I applied, asking for a phone interview. The phone interview went well, and they scheduled another phone interview with the executive director. After that interview I was informed that they would be making their decision within the next couple of weeks.

This entire time I was just praying to God and asking His will to be shown to me. More than anything, Quintin was heavy on my heart and mind. After losing my mom and our family shattering the way that it did, I really wrestled with whether a move to Florida was the right thing to do. When I prayed about it, I felt the Lord say that a move to Florida was the best thing for everyone. That Piper and I needed a fresh start, and Quintin needed to decide, once and for all, how he was going to choose to live his life.

The company offered to fly me down for an in-person interview. I flew down in early March of 2018 and met with the executive director and other staff members. I saw the operation and facility, and of course, felt the warm weather. I do have to say that the interview did not go as well as I had hoped. I had mixed feelings and reservations about working directly with the executive director. There was just something that did not click with us in that interview.

I came back to Minnesota with mixed feelings. Part of me wanted to move to Florida and believed that this is supposed to be a fresh start, but part of me was having serious reservations about the job, and the responsibilities it would entail. So much to my surprise and delight, the human resources director called me a week or so later to let me know that they had decided not to offer me the position, but they knew I was meant to be a member of their team, so they would like to offer me another position within the company within the development department with a very fair salary and compensation package. They informed me that I needed to be able to start by April 2nd.

I knew that God had opened the door and that I was meant to go.

Shortly before I left, I discovered that Quintin had tried using heroin. When I confronted him about it, he admitted to using it once a long time ago but denied using it recently. I explained to him that there was nothing that I could do to help him anymore until he was ready to help himself. I would not give him any money and I would not even be able to talk to him until he was ready to get help. I told him that our relationship had deteriorated to a pile of manipulation and lies, and that his addiction and drug use had more control over him than anything else. He had some harsh words to say and encouraged me to just go to Florida and move on without him.

Despite this, I accepted the job and began to prepare for the move.

I quickly put my house on the market, gave away or sold virtually everything I owned except for what could fit in the back of my car and on Easter weekend 2018, I made the drive down to Florida. After getting there and finding a place to live, Piper came down to join me and we started happily soaking up the sunshine in Florida.

It was not too long after the move to Florida that Quintin reached out, and said, "Mom, I can't do life like this anymore. I don't want to do life my way anymore. I want to just be sober and healthy and happy. I want to be in Florida with you and Piper. Can I move down with you?"

Now as for any parent who has had to walk with a child struggling with addiction, you know that you have had these kinds of conversations, many, many times. There is all the hope and promise in the world, and you have had your heart crushed each time when it does not pan out. So, it was not an instant yes for me. I told him I needed to think about it and pray about it. I knew what bringing him down to Florida would mean for my life and for Piper's life. The little escape we had would now be met with the complexities of Quintin's addiction.

I also hoped that maybe, just maybe, this would be the thing that would make the difference. Maybe getting him out of a state surrounded by painful memories and heartache, removing him from his group of friends, and having him come across the country to get a fresh start, would be the thing to help him maintain sobriety. I rationalized that the worst-case scenario would be if he came down and could not maintain sobriety, I would just plop him into my new place of employment where they had a year-long, faith-based recovery program that had huge success rates.

After a couple days of consideration, I agreed that he could come down and join us. We were all excited about the possibility of him coming down. After talking about it a little bit more, we decided that late July would be the best time for him to come down for him to save a little money, give sufficient notice at his place of employment, and get his car ready to make the trip down. It also gave me time to move into a bigger place that had an additional bedroom for him, which I did.

We talked nearly every day about plans and hopes and dreams for when he got to Florida. He started looking for a job down in Florida and started putting feelers out. He excitedly gave notice to his place of employment and was really happy to be coming down to Florida. I have to say, it was great to have my kid back. I heard optimism for the future in his voice and I saw him thinking and planning again. He began dreaming about a better life. I saw his hope restored.

His father's family in Minnesota decided to give him a going away party for him Saturday July 7. I spoke to him that day on the way to his grandmother's house and he shared with me that he had not decided if he was going to spend the night there or go out with a friend. He shared with me that he intended to have a beer or two at his grandmother's house, which I wasn't thrilled about, but I was not waging that battle.

I encouraged him to stay at his grandmother's house. I told him that the last thing he needed right now was a DUI. They held the party with family and one peculiar guest, a "friend" who came down from St. Cloud (an hour and a half drive) to say his goodbye to Quintin. No one had ever met this "friend" before. He came and stayed for 15 minutes and left.

Later we would find out that this "friend" was the drug dealer who sold him the drugs that would take Quintin's life later that night.

Losing My Breath

The next day was Sunday, July 8. I woke up and went to church. I remember specifically in church that morning, they were talking about a church-wide picnic that would be happening in a few weeks, and Piper's father and I discussed how great it would be that Quintin would be down there in time for the picnic. We were thrilled that we would all be able to go to this picnic together as a family. I went home and had a lovely afternoon. I made some food for the week ahead, and relaxed.

About 6 p.m. that night, Quintin's best friend Michael from Minnesota texted me to ask if I had heard from Quintin that day.

I texted back, "No, why, what's up?"

Then he called me. "Quintin never came home last night," Michael said. "We're just trying to find him."

Now, again, for someone who has a 20 something year old kid that has wrestled with addiction the idea of him not coming home, or not being where he is supposed to be is not out of the ordinary. But it was the fact that Michael was now calling me, and the tone of his voice, that told me something was wrong.

"Michael," I said, "What's *really* going on?"

He said, "Well, somebody posted something on social media and we just can't make sense of it. We don't know why somebody would say that."

I said, "What did it say?"

He forwarded me the post. It was a picture of my son that said, "Gone too soon…. rest in peace."

When I saw it, the air instantly left my lungs. I could not breathe. I fell to my knees. I abruptly hung up on Michael and I sat there in panic and shock. I called my sister instantly.

I could not even speak. I sat there hyperventilating on the phone. Eventually she got me to slow down my breathing enough to tell her what I had heard. We instantly went into fact-finding mode. We called hospitals and police stations. We filed a missing person's report.

Somewhere in the chaos, Michael called me back and explained that they heard he was with a friend in St. Paul, and that he, Michael, was driving around St Paul looking for Quintin's car near the place he was rumored to have been the night before. Eventually he called back to notify me that he did find his car, and it was empty. He was literally going to knock on doors to try to find out where Quintin was.

Not too long after that, Michael called me crying, weeping in fact, saying that he tracked down the people that were with Quintin the night before, and that Q had overdosed.

I instantly thought he had overdosed but not died, so I said, "Well, what hospital is he at? Where is he?"

He said, "He didn't wake up, Kelli. I'm so sorry, he didn't wake up."

Grief hit me again. This time in the stomach. I thought I was going to throw up.

We still, at this point, did not have anything confirmed from anyone other than a bunch of rumors. So, we still were frantically calling hospitals and police departments.

I called Quintin's father, hysterically crying. I left him a voicemail begging him over and over to tell me it was not true.

When he finally got the voicemail, he called me back and asked what was going on. After I told him what had been happening, he said, "No, that can't be true, I just saw Quintin yesterday, he's fine."

I explained more about what everyone was saying, and he said he would make some calls and get back to me.

About 45 minutes later, his father called me back to let me know that the police were at his door and had confirmed that Quintin passed away early that morning.

I threw my phone on the floor and screamed, *"No, no, no, it's too much! It's too much, God, it's too much!"*

Piper and Shane were there by this time. They heard me scream when I got the official news as I sat on my closet bedroom floor. I will never forget Piper's very first words to me after she got there were, "You're not going anywhere, are you, mom?"

This poor kid just lost her grandmother to suicide, and now her brother to overdose. Her first concern in that moment was about my ability to handle the weight of this. "I'm not going anywhere," I assured her.

"Mom?" She said gently, "Remember, God never gives us more than we can handle."

"I wish God would stop thinking so highly of me," I said back.

I Let Go

Most of the next few days are a blur. I remember calling close friends and family to tell them what had happened. Each phone call was filled with crying, screaming and weeping on both ends of the phone. I remember lying awake that whole first night, getting zero hours of sleep.

The next morning, it occurred to me that I serve an awesome, loving God. I serve a God who raises the dead. Nothing is impossible with God. I had always regretted never praying for my mom to be raised from the dead because I was so blindsided by grief. That thought didn't even occur to me. I was not going to make that mistake again.

So early Monday morning, I changed my posture, and I put a call out to every person of faith that I knew to pray for his resurrection.

Meanwhile, we booked flights home and Ashley and I, in shock and despair, and in our zombie-like state, began our trip back home to Minnesota.

I had such hope and faith that I really thought I would land in Chicago and have a message from someone that a miracle happened, and he had woken up.

But I landed in Chicago with no such call.

I got on the next flight that landed in Minnesota, and getting off that plane, the weight of it hit me again, that I had just landed back in Minnesota, and that I had returned to Minnesota because my son was dead.

I almost fell to my knees right there in the airport. I managed to stumble my way out and found myself in my sister's arms. She and my aunt picked us up from the airport.

I wept all the way to my sister's house.

Early the next morning, I could not sleep, so I sat outside, talking to God.

Miracles happen, and I asked God, "Why didn't You raise Q?".

God's answer was to show me Quintin. In that moment, God helped me to see and feel perfectly that Q was where *he* wanted to be. That he was whole and happy, and he wanted to be there. He didn't want to come back.

So, I let him go. In that moment I let go.

Navigating

I had just learned skills for navigating grief with my mother's passing, and now I had an opportunity to put those skills to the test.

Thankfully, in my short time in Florida before his passing, I managed to find my way into an awesome church called Grow Church. One of the desperate phone calls I made that first night was to a pastor at that church to let them know what had happened and that I needed help.

The lead pastor of that church was a woman who had lost her husband several years earlier to a battle with cancer, Tracy Boyd. She had intimate experience with grief. She knew what it was to lose someone you love. She was a gift to me in those early days, to help give me the framework and solid ground that I needed to stand on.

Pastor Tracy said a couple of things that really set the tone and pace for my grieving process. For that, I am forever grateful.

She reminded me of the truth of the situation, that Quintin was not gone, that he is in heaven, and not in some cliched way, but the actual truth that he is alive and well, seated in heavenly realms. That this is not goodbye forever, that I *will* see him again and we will have all of eternity to spend together.

The truth of that statement became a framework that I reminded myself of, minute by minute, and hour by hour, eventually day by day, and week by week.

The other important thing she did for me was to affirm and confirm what I had learned from Immaculee. She helped me to set the expectation that I would *not* be sad for the rest of my life. She shared the hope that healing was available to me through my relationship with the Lord. She explained that when her husband passed away, it took a year and a half of mourning, grieving, and contending for healing but that she could name the actual day and place where she knew she was made whole. She believed the same was possible for me.

I grabbed hold of that word, with all my heart.

I knew that in the Lord, what is available for one is available for another. So, I knew if God could heal this woman in 18 months then I could believe in even faster healing.

I knew that the first thing I had to have was the belief, hope, and expectation that I would get better. Plus, the grounding truth that he was not gone forever. He was seated in heavenly places and that I would be reunited with him one day.

Those two things became the bedrock of my healing journey.

What are the statements, beliefs, and expectations that you need to grab hold of? Remember, it is a journey, a process, and while the path can be accelerated, you cannot skip any steps.

Though I had been given the key to healing, I still had to walk it out, and I am still walking it out to this day.

I will continue to walk those same steps until the day that I'm reunited with him up in heaven.

My son, Quintin Casey.

Nothing is Impossible with God

Several of us, including myself, Ashley, and my sister Vicki, knew right away that we wanted to get tattoos to honor Quintin. Tattoos had kind of become a thing in our family.

Quintin, Ashley, and I already had matching tattoos. Our nickname for each other when we all lived together was "Loon." At some point, the inside joke turned from just being a nickname for each other into the idea that we should all get matching loon tattoos.

Then one Saturday morning Quintin came downstairs and declared, "Today's the day! We're getting loon tattoos!"

I cannot really explain Quintin's enthusiasm and ability to be convincing, but there was just something about him. His dedicated belief was contagious. Before I knew it, I found myself driving us all to a tattoo shop to get loon tattoo.

The three of us became the Loon Gang. Ashley and I pointed out our matching tattoos often. It was obvious to us that we now needed to get a Q tattoo to remember him.

I put the word out that we were looking to get these Q tattoos while we were in town. We had a couple of people respond to our request. We even had one guy offer to come to my sister's house and do tattoos right there for anyone that wanted one. But another friend of mine mentioned a tattoo shop in Wisconsin, nearly an hour away, that had an opening for Wednesday of that week.

I am sure it was the Holy Spirit that prompted me to go to the shop in Wisconsin. I knew I had to go.

The next day, we piled in the car to make the trek to Wisconsin, to get tattoos to honor our Q, my son, my Quintin Casey. Our group walked into the tattoo shop, bleak and somber. The place was empty, and we let the girl at the front desk know that we were there for our tattoos. We explained that we all are going to get the letter Q, and began looking at fonts to try to decide for ourselves what style of Q each of us are going to get.

A young girl walked up from the back room, shook my hand, and said,"Hello! My name is Casey, I'm going to be your tattoo artist today."

I was in shock, and only half aware of anything that came out of her mouth after the name *Casey.*

Ashley looked at me, amazed. "Did you hear what she said? She said her name is *Casey!*" Pretty remarkable! Right?

Next thing we know, two little kids came in running around the tattoo shop, being loud and disruptive. The tattoo shop owner came out, apologizing profusely.

She said, "I'm so sorry! I know it's not appropriate to have my kids here. My babysitter called in sick about 15 minutes before the shop opened, and I had nowhere else to take them. I'm so sorry. I hope they're not a disturbance or disruption to you."

We all nodded to her as a sign of understanding, to let her know it was not a problem.

A couple of minutes later, one of the little kids knocked something over and the shop owner came out and said "*Quintin,* knock it off!"

We stared at each other in shock. I yelled out, "Shut the front door!" in disbelief, and ran outside to cry.

Quintin is not a common name. In fact, in all of Quintin's life, we had only met one other Quintin, and I remember it distinctly because he was so excited to meet another Quintin!

This miracle, that this little tattoo shop held both a *Quintin* and a *Casey* was almost too much to take, and the story does not end there!

Vicki ran after me while Ashley explained to the shop owner why I was crying.

"You're not gonna believe this," the shop owner said, "but *my* name is Kelli!"

There we were in Prescott, Wisconsin, in the middle of afternoon with the shop owner Kelli and her son Quintin, and the tattoo artist Casey. Now, if that is not a sign, I don't know what is! I just felt so loved in that moment, that God would orchestrate such details to let all of us know that we are not alone, that in the midst of this immense pain He's there, He sees us, He is with us, and Quintin is with us.

My Q tattoo for my Quintin Casey, given to me in a
tattoo shop owned by Kelli, with son Quintin present and
tattoo artist Casey in Prescott, WI.

For Ashley and I, the events of the tattoo shop seemed and felt amazing, but not unheard of, because we know the God we serve. But for my sister and my aunt, it was a different story. My aunt is very intelligent and very analytical, and she just could not wrap her head around how it was all possible.

She was still trying to get her head around it the early the next morning, while I was sitting on the couch crying, she came up to me and said gently, "I've been over it a million times, and I just can't figure out. What are the odds of that? It's mathematically impossible."

I smiled through my tears, and said, "You're right, it is mathematically impossible. But it's not impossible with my God."

Here are some of the other "Q" tattoos that friends and family members got in honor of Quintin.

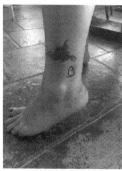

This is a side by side pic of the tattoo that Quintin had on his forearm and a tattoo that Ashley got in remembrance of him.

We flew back to MN and had the same artist that did Quintin's tattoo do Ashley's.

It's ironic to me now because Quintin and I got in a huge fight over this tattoo. He got it when he was 17 illegally from a guy that did tattoos in his house. I was furious that he got a tattoo before being 18. I also thought it was ironic at the time that Quintin never came into agreement with the fact that he had a drug problem, but got the serenity prayer(the addicts pledge of allegiance) tattooed on his forearm.

The Funeral

We prepared for the funeral, meeting with the pastors at our Minnesota church to discuss details. We decided that we wanted the funeral to be open to the public. I wanted Quintin's life to be an example and an alarm for all the young men and women in their early twenties, kids who were messing around with drugs and did not think they had a problem. Like Quintin, a lot of them were taking pills recreationally and did not understand the risks they were taking with every pill. We planned the funeral based on that message.

The funeral was set for Friday the 13th. When we planned the event and discussed who should share what, none of us felt like we would be strong enough to be able to speak, so we intended to leave all the talking to the pastor. We shared with the pastor some stories and things that were on our hearts that we wanted to make sure were communicated.

But the day before the funeral I felt strongly that I wanted to share. This was going to be the one public gathering of everybody who loves Quintin, and there were messages that needed to be heard.

I began to write the eulogy that I would give, praying for the strength and grace to be able to somehow get through it.

Quintin's Gifts

The next day was the funeral. When you go through the trauma of losing a child, you brace yourself and prepare for the worst, but still nothing can prepare you for the feelings that come up. I remember walking into the church and seeing familiar faces, and being embraced by hugs, and then I walked into the sanctuary ... and saw my baby boy's picture displayed on the screen, with the date that he was born and the date that he passed.

Reality hit me hard.

Most of that day and the service is a blur, but I remember so many people coming up and hugging me and saying kind things, or if they did not know what to say, saying awkward things.

I am sure if you have lost a loved one, you have your own list of inappropriate things that people have said, without realizing what they were saying was hurtful.

For example, a business acquaintance of mine, someone that I had known for a few years, who did not know Quintin but had come to the funeral out of respect for me, approached me and pulled me aside.

"So," he asked, "What happened?"

Um ... not exactly the thing to say to a mother at her son's funeral.

Purely by the grace of God, I was able to get through the speech that I wrote, and share my heart with the people in attendance. For a whole bunch Quintin's peers, this was their first encounter with death, their first experience of losing someone their own age, and they were facing their own mortality that day.

They were facing the myth of invincibility that most of us walk in when we are young. They were realizing that that was a lie, and a lot of them were coming to some hard conclusions about their own lives. Many of them were forced to take a long hard look at their own reckless behavior of drug use. We had a handful of people receive salvation that day. We also had several more people come up afterwards and ask for help and prayer with their own issues around drugs.

On the next page is the eulogy I shared at Quintin's funeral.

Thank you for celebrating Quintin's life with us. I am going to be referring to <u>Quintin</u> in the present tense, because he is not past tense. He has not ceased to exist. He is more alive now than he has ever been. He knows no pain, he is experiencing fullness of joy, he is whole. It is in this state that he gets to spend all of eternity. It's not some cliche saying, it is the truth.

Quintin has simply moved to his permanent heavenly home and the reality of that truth brings me comfort. Now, you might have come here because you knew Quintin personally, or perhaps you are here to support someone who is grieving. Whichever camp you find yourself in, I would argue that you are here because Quintin and the Lord would like to offer you three gifts.

First of all, and most importantly, Quintin would like to offer you the opportunity to meet his Lord and savior Jesus Christ. Q knew and loved the Lord. As recently as last weekend, he brought some guys from his work to church. Only a couple of weeks ago he got one of his favorite scriptures tattooed on his arm, Isaiah 54:17 which reads, "No weapon formed against you shall prosper". Because Q is hidden in Christ, this verse is true and not even death can hold him. So if you don't know Jesus-today you have the chance to accept the gift of salvation. There will be time at the end of the service to pray to receive this gift.

Secondly, Quintin would like to offer you the gift of hindsight. Most of us have the opportunity to learn from our mistakes to make sure we don't repeat them in the future. Quintin doesn't get that chance,so now YOU get to learn from Quintin's mistake. Please know that Q would not label himself as an addict even though he struggled with drug use for seven years, and it was when he was in a really good place in life, when he was excited for the future, that an accidental overdose cut his time on this Earth short. Whether you struggle with drug use or not, all

82

it takes is one miscalculation to end your time here. I pray for your sake and for your family's sake that you receive this gift of hindsight and do not touch drugs from this day forward. Life is too precious and beautiful to risk it for a quick high. Please find freedom. Grow up, get married, have kids and live a full life. Do all the things that Q will not get to do. Remember him when you do and remember this gift of Quintin's hindsight that you received today.

The third and final gift that he is offering you today is the gift of perspective. It's so easy for us to lose our way, to let the stresses of this world steal our joy. We can let our worries about money, our work, how we look, or even social media distract us from the only thing that matters, the ones we love. Trust me when I say that is all that matters. No amount of Facebook likes in all the world will give me one more minute with Q.

So put down your phones, people. Stop worrying about comments online, and listen to the comments of the people you love. Be present. Hear their hearts, and share yours. Hopefully you've gotten a glimpse of this perspective as you've contemplated Quintin's passing. That awareness doesn't need to end here. You can take it with you. You can actually live from this point of view.

If you need something to remind you-please take your service program as a reminder. Or if you want to go all in, you can get a Q tattoo, like me. Whatever you do I hope you keep this day and Q in your heart always.

I know that these words had an impact on those who heard it. That speech was the beginning of how Quintin's story began to have an impact on other people's lives.

It gives me deep satisfaction knowing that some good came out of his celebration of life.

There were many in attendance that day, over 300. But there was one mourner that stuck out to me the most.

As Quintin's young friends and mourners began flooding in for the funeral, I said to Quintin's father, "There's a lot of young kids here, I wonder if the dealer will show up?"

"He's right over there," he replied. Quintin's father did not know the young man's name, but he remembered him easily. He was an interesting-looking boy. He had tight, curly orange hair.

I saw him, looked him in the eyes, and instantly turned around and walked away. I could not trust myself not to do, or say, something that I would regret later. I walked away to cry.

Ashley mustered up more poise, grace, and maturity than I think humanly possible in that moment, as she walked up to him and forgave him. She told him he cannot carry the shame and guilt from this, and that we forgive him.

He wept and left the church.

I don't know where he is today, but I pray to God that what happened with Quintin had a profound impact on his life and helped him to change directions.

Another person who was absent from the funeral that day was the young man who was with Q the night he died. This young man was friends with Q from childhood. The two of them partied that night, drinking and taking drugs.

He was the last person to see Q alive.

And it was him who woke up in the morning to find Quintin, blue in the face, and passed away.

He screamed, and his roommates came running in. One tried to resuscitate Q while they called the ambulance.

After the police came and questioned him, Q's friend disappeared the day of Q's passing, and this was part of the reason it took us so long to find out what happened. He is also the reason for the leak on social media. Though he was not the one who shared the initial post that Michael saw that day, he told another friend what happened, and that friend is the one that posted about it.

I was able to talk to Quintin's friend two days after the funeral and forgive him. I released him from any sense of obligation or wrong-doing and told him that I would do everything in my power to help him get help. I told him that he didn't have to live his life struggling with drugs and addiction. He went on to get help, at a local recovery center shortly thereafter, and last time I checked, he's been sober ever since. Another life forever changed because of Q's passing.

These lives that were forever changed was evidence of the beginning of the fulfillment of a request I made of the Lord shortly after Q died.

I asked the Lord for 300,000 lives saved, set free, healed, delivered, or impacted for good, because of Qs story. Pursuing that aim is now my life's purpose. It is the goal, purpose and mission of my non-profit organization, Qs Army, which is entirely focused on helping families that have experienced loss because of overdose. The purpose of Qs Army, of this book, and my own personal mission is to provide encouragement and hope for people currently struggling with addiction and as a preventative measure for young people before they get wrapped up in addiction.

The first annual Qs Army Overdose Awareness Event

August 31, 2019

The Next Season

After the funeral, it was time to go back to Florida, and I honestly did not know how I was going to go back to work at a homeless shelter and addiction recovery center. How was I going to face people that looked like Quintin, every day? I didn't know that I would have the strength to do it, so I told God that I would go and just see how it went.

I went back and was greeted with love and support. I was given the opportunity to speak to the men and women in our addiction recovery program, and share with them the hurt, loss, and pain of a mother who has lost her child to overdose. I was able to let each and every one of them know how loved and cherished and valuable they are, and how devastated we would all be if they were not on this planet.

I was able to show them how broken their mothers would be if they died. I was able to share with them how precious the gift of life is, and the gift of recovery that was being made available to them through the program. I pleaded with them to make use of it and to make the most of this opportunity. To grab hold by the horns and fight their demons head on. I begged them to go on, live their lives and do amazing things. I assured them that sobriety is only the beginning.

I let them know that each one of them was designed for greatness, and all they needed to do was grab hold of that truth for themselves. I extended them an invitation to join Qs Army, to be a part of the 300,000. I informed them that if my son's story has impacted them, that when they go on and do amazing things, it would be credited to Q up in heaven.

That was how I began recruiting for Qs Army and those talks were so healing for my heart.

As time went on, and the more healed I became, the more I realized that my work environment was not a great place for me. The final straw for me was when a handful of the students left the program, only to relapse. My heart was breaking all over again. I was seeing people that I really cared for making reckless decisions with their lives and walking away from the opportunity for help. I could not help but think that I was going to watch them follow in the same footsteps of Quintin. It was too much for me to bare. I cried for three days.

I gave notice at my job and began to seek the Lord about what to do. I carried this burden to help people and to share my story, to be to others what Immaculee had been to me. I had no idea where to begin.

You might as well have asked me to start a career hiking on Mars and I would have felt equally as equipped. Nevertheless, I began reaching out to and walking alongside people who were grieving. I put pen to paper to plot out the things I learned about how to move through grief. I knew I had to put it on paper, because in my search for resources I did not find anything like this. I wish I would have had it for myself!

Having a roadmap is so helpful because one of the toughest things to deal with regarding grief is that it is so disorienting. You get your feet swept out from underneath you. Up is down, and down is up. The five-step framework that we are going to share in the next section of this book was solidified and formed from my conversations with God and from taking action. I had now developed a solid roadmap that people could follow.

As of the writing of this book, it has been a year and a half since his passing. I am walking in joy and peace and contentment with an expectation for good. I am functioning, thriving, and doing amazing things in my life.

I also carry with me the memory, the hurt, and the pain of the loss of my mother and Quintin. The pain does show up from time to time, asking to be let out, and I make room for expression as my soul guides me to, but the pain does not dictate my days. It has not discouraged my dreams. It has not distracted me from my goals in life.

It did not happen instantly, or without considerable effort on my part.

I am here to share my story with you, not to tell you that it is fair, or that it is not hard, or pretend that I can make it all go away. Or to tell you that you will not have hard days, I'm not here for any of that.

What I am here for is to tell you that it can get better, and that there are things you can do to help make it better.

To let you know that when the hard days come, I will stand with you. You do not have to do it alone. You are stronger when you are with other people who understand. I can help keep you pointed in the right direction and moving forward.

That is the purpose of this book. That's the purpose of my message. That will be the purpose of my life for however many years I have remaining on this planet.

With that, I hope that you're ready to begin rewriting your story and learn this framework. To begin embracing and adopting this framework for your own personal benefit, to begin or accelerate the healing process.

Part 2 - Rewriting Your Story: The Five Step Process

I am so excited for this part of the book! I know it might sound strange to say that I am excited in a book about grief, but I am excited because I know how immobilized you can feel and how stuck you can get without these tools.

It is time for you to begin reshaping your story and creating your personal roadmap to restoration.

Let's jump right in with step one of the five step process.

Step 1 Establishing Your Framework

In this step we are going to look at some critical keys to restoring order in your mind and creating the filter through which you will process the rest of the steps.

This is the most important step and the step that will most likely take a little bit more time than the other steps. Please take your time with this. Do not simply skim through this chapter or try to race through this part of the book. As you read this information, sit, reflect, and answer each of the questions that I ask. I give you permission to be 100% real and honest with yourself about where you are, and what you want.

There's no wrong answer here. This is *your journey* and *your choice*. What you determine in this step, will determine where you go, and how fast you get there. The good news of this chapter is that you get to decide *both* of those things; where you want to go, and how fast you are going to get there. So please pour over these pages.

Take time in prayer and meditation to decide for yourself what your answers are and how you want to move forward.

Your framework for processing through this consists of three things:

1. Determining what you believe
2. Deciding what you want
3. Finding an example of someone who has what you want that you can learn from.

What You Believe

Beliefs are a funny thing. I find that most people do not always take the time to consider what they believe. Often beliefs are just handed down from parents, tradition, culture, or society. Most people adopt their belief systems at a fairly young age, without ever having questioned or deciding for themselves if they truly *believe* their beliefs.

Even within the context of religious belief systems there are varying sets of beliefs. There are belief systems about education, finances, relationships, and certainly grief. There are some very prominent belief systems that our culture has adopted as implicit truths. Things that have been handed down for generations and are the main messages that you see out in the world.

We are going to analyze some of those beliefs and you're going to have the opportunity to decide for yourself what you choose to believe about grief.

You get to decide about what this loss in your life means for you.

Questions to Ask Yourself

Take some time to work through these questions. As you reflect, write your answers down in a journal or notebook. I want you to look at this list of questions and really decide what *your* answers are to these questions.

For now, just answer the questions the best you can, and leave the list of answers there whether you feel like your answer was a positive or negative response.

I do not want you to focus on changing your beliefs right *now*, I just want you to become aware of the beliefs that you have.

1. What do you believe about the loss of this loved one?
2. Do you believe that your life is over?
3. Do you believe that you will never see this person again?
4. Do you believe that you are somehow at fault?
5. Do you believe that you will be sad for the rest of your life?
6. Do you believe that it is dishonoring your loved one if you are not sad for the rest of your life?
7. Do you believe that your loved one would want you to be happy?
8. Do you believe that it is possible for you to be happy again?
9. Do you believe that you never recover from grief, but rather learn to live with it?

As you look at the list of your answers and consider your beliefs, consider also: Where did you get these beliefs?

I want you to try to remember at what point you started to believe that belief. Was it a conscious choice that you made to believe the things you believe? Did you intentionally choose to adopt every belief, or is it something that other people have said to you? Did it come to you through messaging that you saw on TV? Was it based on experiences that you had earlier in life? I want you to remind yourself of the place and time when you started believing these beliefs.

I'll give you an example of how this works.

When I lost my mother to suicide, and no one around me could really relate, or understand, I believed that that no one could help me. I came into agreement with the lie that I was all alone, and that this pain was insurmountable. I chose to believe that there was no way I could recover from it and there was no one that could help me. Believing that one lie is what kept me stuck for months and months.

It was not until I heard Immaculee on that stage, sharing her story of surviving the Rwandan genocide and then being healed completely of her grief, that shattered that false belief. It shattered the illusion that no one could understand me. It destroyed the lie that there was no way I could get through it. That was the beginning of my healing process, and what got me unstuck.

That is why it is so important for you to look at your beliefs.

We are going to look to identify if you have any beliefs that are keeping you stuck.

Beliefs can work both ways, negatively and positively, so let's take a look at the effects of holding onto a positive belief.

When my son passed away and I spoke with my pastor, she shared with me that I would recover from this, and how she was completely healed from grief within 18 months of losing her husband to cancer. My choice to believe her, and then to grab hold of her 18-month healing journey and believe that mine would be shorter than 18 months, was *pivotal* in my accelerated healing process. The fact that I embraced those truths within days of my son's passing dramatically changed my course and shaped my path. It determined the amount of time that I was going to be walking in really heavy grief.

Where are you in your process? What do you believe about healing?

I also want to invite you to look at the eternal side of things. I am not here to dictate to you what you should believe about an afterlife. I am here to ask the questions and raise your own awareness of what your beliefs are and invite you to own them. Own your beliefs.

Another example of this belief framework working on my behalf is that when Quintin passed away, I knew that he had moved to heaven; that that was where he was. Not only did I believe that he was made whole in heaven, but also that he was no longer experiencing pain. He was no longer tortured and experiencing the emotional turmoil that he had been experiencing on Earth. His living in heaven also means that I will see him again one day, and that our goodbye is not forever. Even though it may feel like forever at times, I know there's a higher truth I will see him again and we will spend all of eternity together.

The beginning of my personal framework for healing about my son was:

1. The belief that I could get better and be healed from this,
2. The belief that he is seated in heaven and I will see him again

The belief that my son is in heaven was the thing that I reminded myself of moment by moment, then hour by hour, and then day by day. That belief was the thing that I conditioned my mind to meditate on.

Later, we will get a little more into the neurological side of how your brain works, and how to control your thinking, but for now, let's focus on the idea that you *choose* your beliefs.

Turns out, you actually *are* in control of your mind! Your mind and your thoughts do not need to be in control of *you*. You can pick and choose what thoughts you want to think, and the more you think about those thoughts, the more conditioned the choice becomes.

No matter how hard grief shows up in your life, you can train your mind how to respond. You are not waiting for grief to show up, and then trying to figure out how to respond. You are conditioning yourself ahead of time how to respond, so that when it shows up, your response becomes automatic. The fact that you can condition your beliefs and use these beliefs to condition your responses to events are very real things.

You will only rise as high as your belief system. If you believe that you are never going to recover from this, then I am sorry to tell you, my friend, that you are never going to recover from this. If you believe that the pain is going to be as strong 20 years from now as it is today, then that will be your reality.

But that is good news for all of us, because that also means that if you choose to believe that you *can* recover from this, that you can live a full, healthy, happy, productive, joy-filled life, then that is what you will get.

It is okay if you do not feel like that. It is okay if your feelings do not match your thoughts. Feelings are typically the last thing to change. This is a trap so many people get caught in with grief. They let their feelings tell them what they should think, and they let their feelings dictate their actions. It is like the tail wagging the dog.

The way to navigate through this process effectively and efficiently is for you to take control of your mind, and let it know what you are going to think. When big emotions show up, which they will, you are going to decide what you want to do with those emotions. Don't worry, we will get to that in later steps, but I just want to paint the picture here because right now it is imperative that you choose to believe what I am saying.

You need to choose to believe that even though sometimes your emotions feel so debilitating, it is possible for you to learn how to manage your emotions. It is possible for you to learn how to direct and dictate what you are going to do with those emotions. You need to be able to come to a place of believing that it is possible right now, or it will not be possible for you.

Before you go any further, decide what you choose to believe. Take a look at all these areas and get real with yourself about what you believe. Do not go forward until you've done that. Do not pass GO. Do not collect $200. Take as long as you need. Trust me, it is worth it!

Deciding What You Want

The next piece of our framework is deciding what we want. So, in this section we are going to take a good hard look at that process.

A map is only good if you know where you are going. If I have a map of the United States, unless I decide on my destination, that map is just white noise, and not useful to me. I have to decide for myself where it is that I want to go, so that the map becomes active to me. That is what we are creating here, the roadmap to restoration. We are creating the map for you. Even with the awareness of what you believe and with all the other tools that I am going to share with you, if you have not decided for yourself where you want to go, a lot of this information is going to be useless to you.

So, let's talk it through, and think through some of the common things that people may want after they have experienced such a significant loss. Again, this is an invitation for you to look at each of these areas to get honest with yourself and decide what you want. This is where you are selecting the destination on your roadmap to restoration. There are a lot of places that we could go on this map, and some are more fruitful than others, but again you have free will and free choice! We are all incredibly powerful and capable. You get to decide where you want to go.

Here is a list of some of the common things that people may want after they have experienced the loss of a loved one.

- Answers
- Justice
- Vengeance
- What is Fair
- Sympathy
- Peace

All of those are things that you are entitled to. I am not here to tell you that you cannot or should not have any of those things.

I am here to tell you, however, that some of those things are distractions or diversions, and will only keep you stuck.

Let's unpack them one at a time.

Answers

Answers is a big one. When life blindsides us, when something happens that we did not see coming, when sudden trauma or tragedy hits our lives, we just want to know how it happened.

We want to know how we could have missed it. Could we have done anything differently? I know, especially in the case of my mother's passing, the fact that she took her own life, compounded by the fact that my father's story about that night before was sketchy at best, had my mind screaming for answers.

I wanted to know what happened. What was said? Did he know that she had taken these pills? What was she thinking when she died? Was she planning this? Was my dad telling the truth? Did the police do everything they could have done?

Answers, answers, answers.

Our minds, our rational, logical minds, seek to make sense of everything. God built us in a way that we have an amazing ability to put pieces of data together and get them to make sense. We have the gift of logic and rationalization. We make sense of things and we depend on that, day in and day out. We have to make sense of traffic laws, and gravity, and so many things in our world in order to exist.

When the unimaginable happens, our mind is desperate to make sense of it. Our mind is looking at all the dots of information and is looking for a pattern. It's trying to find the logic in it, looking for the reason and the answer.

Our minds are forever trying to make two plus two equal four, and when it does not add up, we get stuck.

Let me affirm you that if you are wanting answers, that it's completely natural. It is a completely natural response to want to understand *why*. It is part of the way that God wired us, and to a certain extent you *should* seek answers. You should ask questions. You should pursue all the information that's available to you to try to appease that reasoning mind.

The part where it can become a trap is when you have pursued and received all the information that is available to you, and you still do not have answers. If you let answers become your goal, you may be stuck there for a long time; possibly, the rest of your life.

Another thing I want to warn you about is, if you choose answers as your destination, you may get answers one day and still not have peace. A word of caution and advice: *really* decide for yourself if answers are what you want. Only you can decide for yourself. When is that stopping point, once you feel you have exhausted all the information that is available to you? Only you can decide that you have all the answers you need.

Justice

Oh, when we feel cheated and wronged, how our hearts and minds cry out for justice! Because, after all, God is a God of justice, right? He wants to see justice done on the earth. He is not a God of injustice. When we have been violated or when our loved ones have experienced injustice, we want justice for them.

This is another thing that tripped me up as it relates to my mother. I was so enraged on her behalf and on my own behalf. I felt that the medical system, the hospital system, and social worker that allowed my father to be released from the hospital, all failed my mother miserably. I felt that the police that came to the scene and did not do any kind of investigation or ask any questions about the circumstances surrounding my mother's death failed my mother miserably.

I felt that my father with his inconsistent story, and lack of love or support that last night, failed my mother miserably. I wanted each and every one of them to be held accountable. As far as the world knows, my mom took her life and that's all there is to the story. That she was a 62-year-old woman who got sad and took her own life. I know there is so much more to the story, and I wanted to scream from the rooftops! I wanted everyone to be made aware of how they had failed my mother and failed me. I wanted them to be held accountable. I wanted them to have to answer for themselves and for the brokenness of the system. I wanted to sue the hospital system. I wanted to sue the county. I was to the point that I almost reached out to media. I was talking to lawyers and trying to pursue this injustice.

The tricky part of the belief that you want justice is that seeking justice feels like progress. Because you are not just sitting still immobilized, you are doing something and it's a way to fight back against this heaviness. It feels productive, but it can also be a trap. The thing you need to weigh out when you're pursuing justice, is what is the cost? Do you know the cost of pursuing justice? Do you know what it will cost you and your loved ones? Do you have the time, energy, and funds needed?

If you have not learned this already, let me clue you into the fact that you need to become acutely aware of your emotional and energetic resources, and be very discerning and wise in how you spend those resources. You do not have an infinite supply. You need to be very wise about what you are giving your energy to, because it is taking a tremendous amount of emotional and physical energy for you to just get up every day.

In my case, as I pursued all these paths to seek justice, I finally got to a place where I really inquired of the Lord to ask if this was a fight, He was wanting me to fight. I had to ask myself if I had the resources to fight that fight well. I sat down and took a long, hard look at what the cost would be to me and my family if I pursued justice on a public stage. I concluded that it was not a fight I was meant to fight. It was a battle for which God had not given me the resources, conviction, or the grace to fight.

Vengeance

So as much as I wanted it justice and vengeance, I had to lay down my wish for vengeance, and trust that vengeance belongs to the Lord. That He sees the injustices of the world and is working all things together for the good of those who love him and are called according to His purposes.

Vengeance is like justice but more personal. Justice wants people to be held responsible, vengeance wants people to feel the hurt they have caused. For a long time, I wanted my father to feel the weight of his sin. I wanted my father to hurt. I wanted my father to feel the hurt that we were experiencing. It took a long time for me to be able to come to a place of letting go of that, and to trust the Lord with my father completely to forgive him. To be able to want him to receive forgiveness, healing, and wholeness.

Turning Unforgiveness Into Forgiveness

If what you want is vengeance, then there is likely some unforgiveness in your heart. Unforgiveness will absolutely keep you stuck.

If you find that you have unforgiveness towards the person that passed away, or towards someone connected to the situation, or even toward the Lord Himself, you need to work through that and stay there until you can get to a place of forgiveness.

There are several ways that you can work on that:

1. Try journaling every day and be honest with the Lord about where you are, and what you are feeling. He can take it.
2. Seek counseling if you need help to talk through it.
3. You can bring it to your support community to process through it, and get their ideas about what has worked well for other people. For me it was kickboxing. I took a kickboxing class and it did wonders for me to work through my anger!

Whatever the process looks like for you, keep looking until you find the place and process that feels right for you!

What is Fair

Fair feels so close to justice and vengeance, but the difference here is justice and vengeance is focused on other people, and fairness is about you. If you are screaming, "This isn't fair!" Then you are now focusing on what's happened to you, and feeling like the world, or God, owe you something.

Oh, I can so relate! As I shared in Part 1, when my mother passed away, I felt so betrayed by God. I explained to Him that I was not going to tithe for at least a year. I felt like I had earned the right to keep the tithe for damages for pain and suffering.

I did not blame God for being the source of the pain, but I definitely felt that He could have, and should have, done something to stop it. I held Him responsible and let Him know that I was not going to tithe. I felt like that was fair.

Maybe it would have been fair, but the thing I want to challenge you with, and the invitation I want to extend to you, is to consider that God wants so much *more* for you than simply what is fair.

What is fair is that Jesus would not have had to die. What is fair Is that all of us would have been held accountable for our sins and shortcomings, and we would not be able to be reconciled to the Father.

But God does not operate in fairness, He operates in what is best. If fairness is the thing that your soul is crying out for, I want to encourage you to lay down what is fair in order to receive God's best.

It is okay if you cannot see it right now, today. It is okay if you do not have the faith to know what that could even look like. How could God deliver more than what is fair? You would be happy with fair at this point, you just want things to be made right. I can understand that it might be hard for you to even conceive of receiving something more than fair because this loss seems so huge and consuming, but I am here to tell you that it is available.

That is what God has for you. That's how He loves us. The problem is that God is a Gentleman, and He works in cooperation with us. It requires our participation and agreement in order to receive what He has for us. So, if all you are demanding of God is what is fair, you literally just put a limit on how far He can move in your life. If what's fair is as big as you're going to reach, then that's as big as God can move.

I implore you, as hard as it may be, as much as it might stand in contradiction, or opposition to your reasoning mind, to lay down your right for what's fair and begin to believe and trust God, for God's best.

Now this next one could poke a lot of people, and that's okay.

If you find yourself getting offended at this next section, check your heart, and take some time to unpack that. You may be a victim of this without even realizing it.

Sympathy

Do you want sympathy? Is that where you want to go? Is that what you are wanting to receive?

This is such a huge one in our society. It seems like these days everyone is looking for a banner to wave to declare their brokenness to the world. Everyone is looking for a label that identifies them as hurt, or broken, or harmed in some way. We want a reason to tell the world that they need to treat us gently and kindly, that they need to tiptoe around us and walk on eggshells.

It is not just people who are grieving, it is people with this condition, or that condition, or this race, or this sexuality, or this mental health disorder. There is so much focus on what we perceive to be wrong with us instead of celebration about what is right with us.

Grief is certainly no exception. In my experience, it is almost worse with grief because people are so afraid of offending someone who's grieving. We get carte blanche when we are grieving. None of the rules apply to us, we are a special kind of hurting. We have been through the unimaginable. Give us our space, and our process because we cannot possibly be held accountable to be anything to anyone else right now because we are grieving.

Now do not misunderstand me; you have been through something traumatic, and you do need to take care of yourself unapologetically. What I am talking about is taking on the identity of a grieving person or the identity of whatever trauma has happened to you. The truth is something awful has happened to you, and it will change you forever. You will be a different person than the person you were before this happened. But the thing that happened is not who you are.

You are not forever, a mother who lost her child. You are a mother who went through the experience of losing her child. That was an experience in your life that shaped you, and changed you, and my hope is with this book you will be changed for the better. No matter who was lost to you, parent, child, partner, sibling, or friend, you are not forever someone who is grieving. You lost someone you loved. But that is not your identity.

Victim mentality is pervasive in the earth. There are scores and scores of people lining up to tell you that you are wounded and broken, and to tell you that it is never going to get better. They are happy to handle you with kid gloves for the rest of your life if you let them.

Honesty Check In

This is gut check and heart check time.

Have you been disproportionately seeking sympathetic attention? Have you been finding your purpose in being wounded? Has your only source of comfort coming from people who tell you how sorry they are for you?

I had so many people come up to me after Quintin passed away and say, "Oh my gosh, Kelli, I don't know how you get out of bed in the morning! I would be in bed all day if I were you." They said it like it was a compliment.

I had to check myself and make sure that I did not come in agreement with their sympathy because if I come in agreement with their assessment, then all of a sudden I have set the bar for myself to just getting out of bed every day. That would become my measure of success. I do not know about you, but I want to do a whole lot more in my life than just get out of bed every day! I want to enjoy my life and do amazing things.

And so, sympathy is a very dangerous thing. It is so prevalent in our society and so many people choose to just live off of the sympathies of others.

Please, by all means, seek support. Have people love on you, but do not allow people's sympathies to define who you are or where you are headed. Do not allow people's sympathies to keep you stuck.

Peace

The last choice on our list of possible destinations is, in my opinion, the best choice, and that is peace. Peace and restoration of joy.

Have you decided that peace is your destination? Then the roadmap you establish is going to quickly bypass all those other places. It is going to help you discern and decide how much time you should spend at any of those other places. If peace becomes the destination, and you pursue answers you will quickly decide when your pursuit of answers is keeping you from peace. You will have the wisdom to know when you have received all the answers you are going to receive and how the continuation of pursuing answers is robbing you from getting to peace.

You no longer have to be confused or wait for anybody else. This destination of peace will become your roadmap and your guard.

I do want to inform you that you may need to lay down your need for all the other things if peace becomes your goal. You may need to surrender your sense of entitlement for all the other things that we have discussed, because the Lord promises peace, in fact, He promises the peace that surpasses understanding, but He also says that all of those other things belong to Him.

Justice and vengeance belong to the Lord. You cannot demand those other things, and demand peace at the same time. You must choose, and friend, please choose wisely.

I promise you, if you make peace your aim, then as long as you lay down all those other things, you will get peace!

You may get all those other things as well, but you will get them in a way that you can sustain them, and it does not violate your peace.

Since I made peace my aim, I have received some of the answers I was looking for, I have received healthy sympathy from loved ones, I have received more than what is fair. I understand that vengeance belongs to the Lord, and I am beginning to receive repayment, but not as the world repays, but the as the kingdom repays. I have been blessed already in this short period of time. I have been blessed beyond measure. I have been blessed with more than I would have asked for myself.

I am only a little over a year into this, so I know that as time goes on, the list of blessings is going to continue to grow and grow and grow.

What you believe and what you want, make up the substance of your framework. The last part of step one is to find an example of someone who is carrying what you have.

Finding Examples

There are coaches for so many areas of our lives. We have coaches to help us get in shape, we have coaches to help us with our finances, and we have teachers who teach all sorts of subjects in school.

But who is coaching us when it comes to grief? Who is showing us, by example, how to do this well? Who is demonstrating the day to day practical tips? This is why I am doing what I am doing.

Because in my journey with grief, I did not find great examples. I did not find people out there who were even telling me it was possible that I could recover. Much less, showing me how to do it.

When I saw Immaculee in the beginning, she proved to me it was possible, and that alone was enough to motivate me to search for the resources and tools that I needed to get there on my own.

However, it is so much easier if you can find people to follow. Whether it is one person, or multiple people. I hope that I am to be at least one example in your life, and that by reading this book you are seeing an example of someone walking in freedom!

You are seeing an example of somebody who is healed, and you can believe that it is possible for you. I encourage you to seek out other examples of people who have done this well.

Interlude...

God is so good. The way that I wrote this book is to go for walks and dictate into my phone. I find that it is much easier to just talk to you than to write.

One of the ways Quintin shows up in my life is that sometimes, I see the car he had when he passed away, a grey Kia Soul. As I am walking along the road writing this chapter, a grey Kia just drove by.

Quintin apparently says, "Hello!"

That is an example right there, of looking yourself for the little kisses from heaven.

What are the little signs of encouragement that you can see and look for with intention? For me, it is grey Kia Souls. What is it for you? Once you know what it is, be intentional to look for those things and you will find that they will show up right at the right time.

It will become a source of ongoing encouragement for you!

More on Examples and Role Models

Hopefully I can be an example for you. Hopefully you can look to find examples in your own community. If not, literally Google search to try to find examples and role models.

I added an entire section in my course, Advancing Through Adversity, called The Champions of Advancing Through Adversity. I rounded up about a dozen people that had been through significant loss and were healed, whole, and walking in freedom. I interviewed them to get their thoughts, and tips, and what they would say to you.

It is one of the things I am most excited about with the course, because you can go in and watch those videos every day if you need to. You can see examples of people who have done it, people who've been through what you have been through. We interviewed people with all different kinds of loss. People who have lost a sibling, spouse, child, or parent. We have people who have lost loved ones to suicide, to overdose, to a car accident, to illness.

I wanted every person who purchases the course and goes through the program to have an extensive library of people that they can learn from.

That is also why we created our Facebook community. To be surrounded by people who are doing the thing. People who have been through significant loss but are intentional in choosing not to stay stuck. They are not going to gather once a week and be sympathetic towards one another and stay stuck in a place of sympathy, but they are going to be supportive, understanding, and encouraging to make sure that you keep moving forward.

Your Framework

So, to review, your framework for processing through grief consists of three things:

1. What You Believe
2. What You Want
3. An Example or Role Model

This is the framework through which the rest of the steps will operate. Once you have these three things clear in your mind, I want you to write them down several places. I want you to write them on note cards and have them with you, to be able to read them at a moment's notice.

You should have them committed to memory, but I also want you to have them written on cards because when you read them out loud, you are training your brain.

This is the beginning of your neurological conditioning and training your brain what to believe. You are training your brain how to respond. At times you are going to be able to say your framework from memory, and at times your brain is not going to remember clearly, and you will be able to read it.

This is the beginning of you, taking back control. This is the beginning of you, telling your mind what's up!

My Framework

The framework I created after Quintin passed was:

1. He's not gone, he's just not here.
2. I will see him again in heaven, and
3. We will have all of eternity to spend together.

Those sentences became my mantra. The thing that I would say and repeat over and over. I would even respond to other people if need be, if anyone wanted to project their grief or beliefs on me. I would respond: "He's not gone, he's just not here. I will see him again. and we will spend all of eternity together."

That is my framework, and I think it is a pretty darn good framework, so you are certainly welcome to adopt my framework as your own if you find it helpful. But remember, this is *your* framework, *your* process, *your* journey, and it will be *your* outcome, so you have to decide what framework works best for you. You need to believe in it. Even if you do not feel like you believe in it at the beginning, you need decide for yourself, and choose what you want to believe.

There's a place in scripture (Mark 9:23-25) where a father asked for prayer for his son, and he said, "…if you're willing, or if you can."

Jesus confronted him about his unbelief, and the man replied, "Please help me in my unbelief." So do not get hung up thinking you cannot write something down because you do not feel like you believe it right now. Choose what you want to believe, choose what you want, write it down, and trust that we are going to help you with the belief that as you move through this process it is going to become more and more formed in your mind.

I am so excited for you!

Your Journey

I hope that you've taken prayerful time with this chapter. I hope that you have considered the questions and answered the questions honestly. You are on a journey, and it is a process. You are going to begin to move forward, you are going to begin to see improvement. You are going to begin to have movement, and you are going to get where you have decided that you want to go.

I am so thrilled for you, so thankful that you are doing this hard work that you are facing this giant that's in front of you. You are not shrinking back, you are moving forward on purpose, in purpose!

Step 2: Protecting Your Framework

Before we start on this chapter, I want to take a minute to acknowledge and congratulate the work that you have just done! Most of the heavy lifting has been done. You are going to find that the more solidified the first few steps of this process become, the quicker and more easily you are going to move through the rest of the steps and reach your destination.

Let's buckle up as we move through these next sections as you continue to gain momentum, energy, and clarity.

By now you have a very solidified understanding and framework established, one that you are holding on to and filtering everything through. You may find over time as you continue on through the process that your step one is going to become more and more clear, and you're going to be able to lean on it and trust it the more you move through this process.

Now we must learn how to protect the framework. You need to protect it from two primary sets of influences: external influences, and internal influences.

External Influences

As we discovered in Step 1, there are all sorts of thoughts, ideas, theories, and "conventional" wisdom floating around out in the universe as it relates to grief. Since you have taken the time to intentionally choose for yourself what you want to believe, and where you want to go, you need to make sure you do not follow people that are going to a different destination.

For example, if you picked peace as your destination, you want to be careful to not follow the crowd that is demanding answers or justice, or the folks that are looking for sympathy. You need to recognize that not everyone is trying to go where you are going.

The next step is to identify and categorize all information that comes towards you within the context of your framework. All people that you interact with, all messages that you are receiving through media in its various forms, be it TV, print, social media or music. It is time to be intentional about what you are going to allow to come through your gates, meaning the gates of your eyes, the gates of your ears, and the gates of your mind.

This is such a vital process. It is something that most people do not do in life, but this is going to be a huge factor in how fast you recover. We need to evaluate the information that is coming in because if you are continually processing the wrong type of information, or information that is not supportive to your framework, it is going to slow down your journey. If you are trying to go to California, but you are constantly reading a mapping system for Colorado, it is not going to be helpful to you.

Let's look at the different types of external influences you will encounter along your way.

Television and Movies

If you have decided that you want the restoration of peace, it probably would not be very helpful to watch TV shows filled with crime, drama, and murder. It might also be a good idea to limit or remove medical crisis and drama shows for a while.

A perfect example of this in my life is before the addiction issues with Quintin, I used to watch the show *Intervention*. I used to watch it because addiction is so prevalent in my family, and I could relate to what the families were going through. If I am being honest with myself (and you), I liked watching it, because in most cases, the families on those shows were in more extreme situations than I was in, and it made me feel better about my life and what I was facing.

But now I know I will never watch that show again. That show is not in alignment with my framework of having peace and living a healthy, productive, positive, joy-filled life. That show would be a painful reminder of what I have experienced, or it would be a painful reminder of the positive outcome that our family did not get to experience. For me, *Intervention* is permanently removed from my watching itinerary. I find myself watching less and less TV in general, because I can find more positive and productive things to do with my time, but that is a subject for a different book.

You will find that some things are going to be removed off your list for a season, and some things need to be removed off your list permanently.

This chapter is focused on taking an inventory of all those different areas of your life and spending some time thinking through what do you need to limit right now? What do you need to remove right now? Is that just for now or forever?

Here are some things you may want to limit or remove during this season as you are healing:

- News Coverage
- Horror or suspense movies that involve death or dying
- Medical Drama Shows
- Family Dramas
- Depending on the type of loss, shows that talk about drug use/addiction/suicide

Selective Viewing

Here's another tip: be sure that you know what you are about to watch. I remember when the movie *A Star Is Born* with Lady Gaga and Bradley Cooper came out, I saw the commercials and thought, "Oh, that looks like a nice movie about two country singers falling in love."

I decided to go see it based on the 30 second commercial I saw. I took my daughter with me and we went to watch this "love story" that ended up being entirely about addiction and culminated in the suicide of a main character at the end. We sat there, weeping silently and trying to stifle our sobs in this movie theater as this movie poked just about every wound we were carrying in our hearts.

Learn from my mistake. Do not just blindly watch some TV show because it comes on or go to a movie because somebody invites you. Be intentional and proactive to make sure you know what it's about and decide for yourself whether it's going to be good for you or not.

Replacement Viewing

Now this step is not just about eliminating or removing the things that are not in support of your framework, but it is also about filling your time and mind with things that *are* in support of your framework. I highly recommend watching funny movies or lighthearted things that are going to make you laugh or watching movies and television shows that you know make you smile.

Music

You will also need to monitor the music you are listening to. When you pay attention to the lyrics of songs or the vibe of songs, you would be surprised how many contain underlying messages about death, dying, or drugs.

Sometimes it is not an offensive song or lyric, but maybe that the song can take you back to a specific memory or a painful thought. The psychological term is being triggered. I don't like the term triggered because it implies that someone's pulled a gun on you and forced you into some sort of response that you have no choice about. We are working to recognize that we are not victims or captives to our thoughts and emotions, so I do not like to use that terminology. We can just be mindful that things may affect us and influence us. With that information in hand, we can preemptively avoid that circumstance by controlling the things we can control.

Now, we cannot control everything, but it's all about the things that we can control. If you will take the time and energy to control the things we are discussing in this chapter, you will find that you do not get triggered nearly as often because you're going to minimize or remove those things that might trigger you.

Social Media

Recently, I joined several grief groups on Facebook in order to get more in touch with the population that I serve.

At first, it was informative to hear what people are struggling with. I wanted to get a better feel for the scope of how many people are struggling and stuck in grief. I quickly noticed after several days, that seeing this constant feed of people who were overwhelmed and desperate started to take a toll on my mental well-being. I noticed that it was definitely affecting me and my mood. I kept myself in the groups, but I unfollowed several of them so that my Facebook feed does not fill with stuff that is heavy or bringing me down.

That is an example on how to manage social media to meet your needs. Facebook is a great place to start. Just look at your feed. The best thing you can do is unfollow people, you do not have to unfriend them. If someone is putting negative stuff out into the world, or thoughts that do not align with your framework, stop following them. You will be amazed at the amount of energy that you will get back from removing that mental clutter!

People

I want you to make an inventory of the main people in your life, the people that you interact with and talk with the most: coworkers, friends, and family.

I want you to honestly judge and rate how you *feel* after talking to them, whether you feel uplifted or heavier after you talk to them. This is not a place of judgment, shame, or condemnation. You are not saying any of these people are bad people, you are just taking responsibility for your mental health and well-being. You are becoming aware of the things that feed your soul and the things that deplete your soul.

Make a list of the 10 to 20 people closest to you and decide which ones you need to minimize or remove during this season. Give yourself permission not to answer the phone, return a message, or feel the need to engage. This is a time for you to learn radical self-care. It is about you creating boundaries that promote self-care. You get to, and need to, decide who is going to have access to you during this season. Please make those choices wisely!

Just like all the other areas, while it is important to reduce or eliminate the people that are destructive or bringing you down, you need to make sure that you also have enough people that are uplifting, encouraging, and supportive.

A few of the right kind of people will do more for you than a lot of neutral people. Or even worse, a few of the wrong people.

Do not buy into the lie that you owe people access to you. You are a valuable commodity and not everyone needs to have access to you. If someone is not helpful for your healing process, take the necessary precautions to safeguard yourself and your heart. You only need to focus on healing.

Limiting Communication When Necessary

The pastor that I spoke with shortly after Quintin passed away said that for the entire first year after her husband died, she did not answer her phone. She was so intentional about seeking the Lord, studying scriptures to heal her heart, and listening to uplifting music that it was like medicine for her. She found in the beginning, that a phone call would interrupt her and more often than not, the person on the other end of the phone would want to project their grief on her, so she decided to just stop answering the phone all together. She reasoned that she could always listen to a voicemail later, on her time, and return the call if she felt up to it. Now that is radical self-care!

Support Systems

It is imperative that you have a good support system, and that your support system may need to come from places other than your immediate family members. One thing that I realized in my mother's passing, and then again especially with my son's passing, was that all my family had their own grief process to go through. It was not fair for me to lean on them as a main support system for my grieving because they were trying to navigate their own grief. We were all just doing what we needed to do to keep our heads above water. Some of the people that I would normally turn to as a help when times get tough, were not emotionally available to me. I had to get resourceful and find people outside of that network.

One great idea, especially in the early stages after losing someone you love, is to find one or two support coaches or friends that can walk with you. Someone who is a little bit removed from the situation, who can be there for you to help you to process things or just sit there with you. They can help you to process information, paperwork, and everything else that comes with losing a loved one. If you have not done that already, I encourage you to find one or two people to fill that role.

It is vital that your support system knows about the framework that you have established, and that they are in agreement with it. At the very least, if they are not in complete agreement, they are able to support the framework that you are working with.

Ideally, you would find one or two people that are in agreement with your framework that can help encourage you and hold you accountable to what you have committed to doing. That is another reason why we created the Facebook community, because it is sometimes hard to find those people in your day to day life. If you do not have examples of that in your own life, I invite you to join our Facebook community. Spend some time to get to know people. Find a couple of people that can be that for you and do that for you within the context of our community.

Step 3:Protecting the Framework from Internal Influences

Now that we have established the framework and learned how to protect it from external influences, it is time to shift our focus inward and learn how to protect it from our own thoughts and emotions. Thoughts and emotions that show up uninvited and threaten to steal your peace. They steal your joy and zap your energy. Part of what we have been doing already this whole time is conditioning your mind to be able to protect the framework. In this section I want to dig a little deeper to reveal exactly what that means and what that looks like.

See, our minds are *always* changing. Every day, cells are being renewed and regenerated. Neural pathways are being created and being removed from our mind. Our minds and bodies are built just like a computer, and just like the predictive texting capabilities on your phone, your mind is built that way to remember your preferences and patterns. The more you think a thought, the more you meditate on a thought, the more deeply ingrained that thought gets wired into your brain.

The good news for us is, no matter how we feel today, we do not have to stay that way. We can choose to rewire our brains. We can *choose* the thoughts that we think. We can create the perfect environment for healing and wholeness, peace and joy.

Think back to Step 1. When we chose what we believed and what we wanted our destination to be, we began to rewire our brains. Every time you read your framework statement, every time you say it out loud, every time you think about it, you are making that road a little bit deeper and a little bit wider. You are training your brain how to think. The more you do this, the easier it is going to be to deflect or redirect any overwhelming negative thoughts and emotions when they show up. The more ingrained your framework is, the easier it is going to be to deflect things that come against it. But it does not happen overnight. It is a process. That is why it's so important to commit to your framework and meditate on it.

That is also why Step 1 is so imperative and why we did not rush it, because you were literally choosing how you were going to redesign your brain going forward. This is like brain surgery without the knife.

The thoughts that we think and the actions we take are more a result of these new neurological pathways that our new thinking has established.

Did you know that more than 40% of the actions that you take every day are not even a conscious choice? They are a result of you exercising a habit. Your brain and body remember your habits. Muscle memory is a real thing and it starts at the thought level. The things that you think about create a pattern, a process that your body learns and repeats automatically without your awareness.

Conditioned Responses

Let's look at this in the negative context. If every time you see a picture of your loved one who passed away, your conditioned response is to think about the fact your loved one is gone, which brings you back to the memory of the day of the loss, and all those painful memories you are creating a habit. Because the emotions are so powerful, if that is the tape that you choose to play, you are going to feel like you are reliving that, time and time again.

You will be creating a harmful pathway in your mind. Your physical body will continue to feel the hurt, pain, and trauma that you experienced the day of the loss. You will be flooding your mind and body with harmful thoughts, emotions, and hormones.

So many people say that the pain of a loss hurts just as badly today as the day it happened. The reason they feel that way is because that is the tape that they have chosen to play. That is the road that they have chosen to pave in their brain, to consistently revisit and relive, and revisit and relive it over and over again.

Your mind does not know the difference between what you are revisiting in your brain, and what is happening in real life. That is why visualization is such a powerful tool. That is why when people dream, it can feel so real. In fact, people have learned to play musical instruments or do other sophisticated things entirely in their mind, because our bodies don't know the difference between something we are imagining, and something happening in real time.

Your abilities to imagine and recall are so powerful that it is important for you to understand how to use these abilities to your advantage, and not your detriment. Now, I am not suggesting that you can erase bad things from your memory. The fact that your loved one died, and the memory of that day, is very real. What I am suggesting is that you get to choose how many times, how often, and how long you're going to feel the emotions and the weight of it. Now you understand that every time you do, you are making that pathway stronger.

You are making that conditioned response stronger.

When something triggers you and you respond negatively, you are teaching your brain to go back to the painful moment which then releases adrenaline, cortisol, and all the hormones you have been working so hard to rebalance. Every time you choose to do that, you are re-injuring yourself.

You cannot always control the thoughts that enter your mind, but you can control how long you entertain them. One suggestion is to literally set a timer for 5, 10, or 15 minutes if feelings of sadness or grief show up. When the timer goes off, get up, go for a walk, do something to change the thought pattern that is developing. I am not asking to pretend that you do not have sorrow or emotions surrounding the death of a loved one, I am however, suggesting you decide how and when to make room for those emotions in your day to day life.

Now conversely, if you have conditioned your mind to your framework, you will have a very different experience and response.

Let's use mine for example. My framework is that Quintin is not gone, he is just not here. I will see him again, and we will have all of eternity to spend together. That is what I have conditioned my mind to meditate on. That is my automatic response. When emotions come in strong, and some days it's easier than others, but even when they come in very strong, I can redirect by choice to my framework and command and demand my thoughts and emotions align with my framework.

I'm going to give you one example of when I really experienced the power of this firsthand. This was the moment I discovered that this works.

I was driving home from work about a month after Quintin died, and as I was driving home, suddenly, out of nowhere this wave of panic came over me.

The only thing I could hear in my head was HE'S GONE, HE'S GONE, HE'S GONE.

Panic started to take over my body, my hands gripped the steering wheel and I started hyperventilating. I was having trouble focusing on the road. This loud screaming voice in my head just kept repeating HE'S GONE. It hit me like a two by four.

Thankfully, I had my framework already established by that point, so I gripped the steering wheel, and I said back out loud, sternly and firmly, "He is not gone! He is just not here. I will see him again, and we will spend all of eternity together."

In an instant, I mean the very second that I finished making that statement, all the panic left my body. I was completely back to a place of calm and peace. I was able to drive home the rest of the way without issue.

That is the power I am talking about!

That is the power that we all possess. That is what is available to each and every one of us. That is what most people never tap into. Many people, when confronted with the idea that they have the ability to direct their emotions related to their grief, get offended. Those people believe the lie that grief is just too big and that there is no way you can take control of the emotions associated with it.

If you find yourself being offended by what I am saying right now, I want to ask you to think about it, or reconsider. Because I am living proof that this is possible. This is available to everyone. This skill will not only help you to continue to navigate through grief more efficiently, but this skill can be applied to other areas of your life as well. When mastered, this skill is going to allow you to create a life you could have only imagined.

Using These Abilities

Imagine not being overwhelmed by financial stress, work tensions, or relationship issues. Imagine that you could cultivate and master this skill to decide for yourself what you believe and what you want.

Imagine you could condition your mind to respond positively all the time, regardless of what gets thrown at you, regardless of other people's actions, regardless of whatever circumstances come your way.

This, my friend, is the key to living above your circumstances.

This, my friend, is the key to abiding in peace. This is the process where you learn to take your thoughts captive and be in control of yourself once and for all.

More and more scientific studies are being done that affirm and confirm this magnificent ability in our brains. The fact that our brains are not static, that they're ever changing and evolving and they're now linking more and more illnesses to your thought life. Pioneers like Dr. Caroline Leef and Paul G Stoltz are doing some amazing research to scientifically prove these theories.

The latest studies show that over 90% of illnesses can be traced back to your thought life.

Regardless of what happens to you, regardless of what environment you live in, regardless of your genetic expression, what you choose to think about what you choose to meditate on is what makes the biggest difference.

How do we begin to condition our mind positively? Here is a list of tools to get you started:

- ☐ We have already been implementing a powerful one by **establishing your framework and meditating** on it.

- ☐ Writing out your framework statement and **reading it multiple times a day** will help to strengthen and fortify it in your mind.

- ☐ Infuse **joy and laughter** into your life daily
  - o Watch funny clips or videos
  - o Ask a friend to tell you a joke
  - o Laugh out loud, even if it isn't genuine laughter when you start, soon you will be laughing at yourself laughing!

- ☐ Implement **Daily Schedule Structure**
  - o Go to bed and wake up at the same time everyday
    - ☐ This will help to restore the chemical balance in your brain and will also help with restoring a normal sleep schedule

- ☐ Review **what worked and what did not work** each day
  - o Take five minutes before you go to bed to review how the day went, what worked and what did not.
  - o Take mental note, or even better write it out.

- o **Remember that you have never done this before, so you are a student that needs to practice and learn how to do this well**

- ▢ Practice **Self Soothe Skills** Daily
    - o Take a bath
    - o Go for a walk
    - o Talk with a friend
    - o Get a massage
    - o Prepare/eat meals you enjoy

- ▢ Daily **Thought Control Exercise**
    - o Every morning when you wake up, take a blank piece of paper and draw a line down the middle of it.
    - o On the left-hand side of the paper you care going to title it: *Things I can't control*
    - o On the right-hand side of the paper you care going to title it: *Things I can control*
    - o I want you to fill in both sides with the things in your life you can't/can control

Here is an example

- Can't Control

  - My son died
  - My family is emotionally unhealthy
  - Other people's reactions to my choices

- Can Control

  - My response to what has happened
  - The people I choose to surround myself with
  - What foods I eat to promote balance and health
  - The choice to move my body and exercise to release positive hormones
  - The thoughts I chose to agree with and meditate on
  - What I watch on TV, read, or listen to
  - My self-care:taking a bath, going for a walk, talking to a friend

Those are just examples to get you thinking. This is your list and your process.

Now, once you have the lists complete, I want you to look at the list of things you can't control and recognize that they are real, and they suck. Put a limit on how long you look at that side of the list, for no more than 15 minutes. Seriously, set a timer. Then, when the time is up look at, meditate on, read out loud the right-hand side of the list and make a commitment to yourself that you will spend the rest of the day focusing on that side of the list.

This is a POWERFUL exercise.

We are not trying to minimize or pretend that something awful has not happened. That is not what this is about. I know more than anyone that this is a very real loss you have experienced, and that you are trying to work through it.

What we are working on is putting it in its proper place. We are going to position it in your mind so that it allows you to move forward in a meaningful way. This is the hardwiring that is going to help you deal with the overwhelming thoughts and emotions that accompany grief. Initially you are going to have to conscientiously choose how to respond, but soon you will find that your brain is going to start doing it automatically. Your brain is a powerful weapon, and you can train it. Your ability to do this, and your commitment to learn how to master this skill will change you and your life forever.

Step 4:Define Your Community

We are now rapidly moving through this process!

My hope and prayer is that the heaviness, the weight of your grief, is lifting. You are starting to move again. You're starting to pick up speed, and gain momentum. You can see a light at the end of the tunnel, and it is not an oncoming train! It is the light of a new day breaking. It is the light of possibilities. The light of joy coming back into your life.

In this chapter, we are going to talk about the importance of community. We need to be able to identify for ourselves a good community versus a bad community for us in this season. I am going to give you the tools to be able to discern for yourself the community that is going to help you versus the community that is going to hurt you or keep you stuck.

First of all, let me just say that community is so important. None of us are an island. We were built to live in relationship with one another. That's why it hurts so much that the person you love is gone, because we are designed to live in connection. We are designed to be interdependent and connected to one another. God designed us to need one another, to be enriched by having community in our life. There is almost no more important time in your life for you to have a supportive community than when you are facing extreme adversity and walking through grief.

Now I know the tendency for a lot of us is to isolate, especially as more time goes on, it seems like everyone else in your life goes back to living and you can be still consumed with the thoughts and the pain of losing the one you love. I want to encourage you to not isolate yourself in those times, and not to move away from people, but to move closer to people. You need to be discerning about the type of people that you move closer to and operate in wisdom, for your sake, and for their sakes.

Support Groups

Support groups can be an amazing tool. There is something very healing and rewarding about connecting with people who understand your pain. Finding the people who are walking through a season like yours can do tremendous things for you, especially if the loss was traumatic or tragic.

For example, in the case of my mother's suicide, I found that my circle of friends had no context for what I was walking through. They did not know how to be there for me. They did not know what to say and quite frankly, just could not relate, so I sought out a support group.

I went to a suicide support group, and I was initially comforted by the fact that everybody in that room understood my pain, everybody in that room understood the weight of it. They understood the confusion, anger, and frustration. But after I went a couple of times, I noticed that everybody in that room was not really living outside of that room. They had not moved on. There were people in there that had lost their loved one years prior, and they still showed up every Tuesday night to relive, rehash, and remember the painful day of their loss.

Without knowing it, they were conditioning their minds to stay stuck. They were rehearsing, reliving, and dredging up the hurt and the pain. They were wiring their minds for the hurt and pain over and over, again. They justified it all because there were other people in the room that were feeling the same way. They were feeling that it was normal and expected to be hurting that long. Every week they would show up to reinforce their pain all under the premise of supporting one another.

I think that they would be sad to learn that they are causing each other to stay stuck. This is the danger and the trap of some support groups.

Nothing is wrong with support groups inherently, but if there is no victory, if there is no growth, if there's no moving forward, if the constant focus of the support group is restating the pain, then that is not my definition of support.

I am not saying that you should not pursue a support group, or in our case, an Encouragement group, but what I am saying is to be very discerning when you go to go check out that support group.

Gauging a Support Group's Level of Support

- [ ] Has there been any empowering testimony?
- [ ] Are people stating how the group has helped them heal?
- [ ] Do the members seem to have peace?
- [ ] Are they saying they are any better today than they were a year ago?
- [ ] Are they walking in victory and freedom?
- [ ] Is anyone in that room happy?

If the answer is no to those questions, friends, turn around and walk out. Do yourself a favor and do not subject yourself to people who, knowingly or unknowingly, have committed themselves to staying stuck.

The analogy I like to use is this. If you were trying to lose weight, it would not be smart for you to go out every week, and hang out with people who are overweight, eat pizza, and talk about how it's so impossible to lose weight. That would not be a good use of your time. That would not support you in your goal to lose weight.

This is no different. If you have decided for yourself the destination of your map is the restoration of peace and joy in your life, then you need to find people who have peace and joy. You need to find people who have experienced grief, but who are operating in a place of peace and joy. In my experience, those people are few and far between.

That is why I feel compelled to do the work that I do. Because in my search for examples, mentors and role models of people who have successfully walked through grief, I couldn't find many.

I found Immaculee, thank God, and that one woman was enough for me. That one example was enough for me to decide what I wanted for myself, and even if I did not have a support group, or a mentor to closely walk behind, I was going to figure it out.

I did figure it out, and my aim for you is to have both the example in front of you and the tools you need to get back to a place of peace and joy quickly and faster than I did. Why not? You guys have a huge head start on me. You have my example as well as other people's examples on our You Tube Channel (The Grief Guru) to encourage you, plus all the tools that we are mapping out in this book.

This is why I've been on a mission to seek out and find the other people who are walking in freedom and share their stories and testimonies, because we need more examples people who are healed and whole, instead of people who are defending their right to be broken.

Our Community

This is also why I knew it was important to create a community around this book, around the teaching and concepts, because we desperately need to have people around us to encourage us and support us. We need to have people hold us accountable to what we have committed to. Whenever you grow in any way, whenever you make any change, it is so much easier to do when you have support. When you align yourself with people who are going after the same thing. That is why we created the Facebook community @thegriefguru.

Our general Facebook community is for anyone and everyone, whether you've ever purchased a product or not. You can find encouraging support through the Grief Guru community. We have additional smaller groups available for people that go through our Advancing Through Adversity course or join one of our mastermind coaching groups. These are filled with the people that have said, *I am going to move forward on purpose, in purpose. I am going to take this awful thing and learn how to use it for my good.*

You do not have to plug in to our community, but please be committed to finding the right community for you. Do not settle for the grief group at your church if they are not teaching victory in that place. (Or, tell your church they should start an Advancing Through Adversity group there and teach this framework!)

Be an advocate for yourself.

There is value in local face-to-face community, and by all means, if you can find a healthy community in your area, please do that. But if you are in need of community and want support, I invite you to join us on Facebook.

We are better together. Always.

This is something that is not a luxury in my opinion, it is not optional. If you are not part of a healthy community that is helping you with grief, then give yourself a deadline. By the end of this week, take a step to do research online, or go visit a group in your community, or connect with us on Facebook. Get surrounded by community.

There will be days when you just need other people to hold you up. I am walking in healing, peace, and joy and grief still shows up for me. There are times and days when I need to sit with it. When I can discern that my soul needs to have expression. There are days where I need to just feel the absence of my mother and my son, and let my soul express itself.

My son's 22nd birthday was the second birthday without him, and I assumed it would go as the first birthday without him had; a fun day celebrating him, with family, seeing signs of him everywhere. In fact, I planned the launch of my video course on grief to coincide with his birthday which I thought would be a nice way to honor him.

Little did I know that I would spend most of the day crying!

That day I had an amazing group of people come around me and love on me. They encouraged me and motivated me. They told me that it was okay to cry, but to keep moving through my tears. I felt so loved that day, and I knew that community is an important piece of this curriculum. The community we are building will be a people who will come alongside and lift up each other on the days when you need it.

I am not here to tell you that you are never going to cry, or you are never going to be sad, or that it doesn't take strength to do that.

Something that the Lord showed me that day is that sometimes strength looks like walking forward, and sometimes strength looks like sitting still.

You need to know yourself, and know what you need and when, and be surrounded by a community that's going to support you. It took a lot for me to sit still that day, and just let the emotions come and have their expression. That was strength manifested that day. I made forward progress that day because I believe a deeper level of healing occurred.

I'm so thankful for the community that surrounded me that day, and had it not been for them, who knows, maybe I would still be sitting and crying.

I hope you are grasping the value of a community that encourages you, supports you, and holds you accountable. Community that lifts your hands when you cannot, who sits with you when you need to sit, and walks with you when you are ready to walk, and remind you that you are designed for walking. You can't sit too long, or your muscles are going to atrophy.

If you cannot find it in your own area, and if for whatever reason our community is not right for you, then go create your own community. That is what I did. I could not find the community that I needed and wanted, so I am creating it. If you think there is something missing, then chances are it is missing for others as well and your community could fill that.

This community is an expression of what I wish I would have had in that moment.

Step 5: Find a Purpose for Your Pain

Well, here we are! We have arrived at the last step. This last step is something that will continue to unfold for the rest of your life.

The last step is finding a purpose for your pain.

I am a firm believer that everything that happens, both good and bad, is not just for us, but for those around us. Those in our spheres of influence are meant to benefit from the good things that happen to us and are meant to share the lessons learned from the bad things we encounter.

Finding a purpose for your pain is the most rewarding part of the journey. It is where adversity turns into advantage. It is the manifestation of God working all things for good for those who love Him and are called according to His purposes. This is where the awful things can become awesome things. Not that that thing itself is awesome, but that the results of it can be awesome.

This is where Quintin's life becomes Qs Army.

This is where going through the loss of my mother and Quintin becomes this course, this book, and helping others.

Finding Treasures Within Tragedy

In this chapter. We are going to look back to reflect and identify the purpose for our pain. We are going to look at the ways that it has made us better. We are going to embrace the opportunity to make those around us better, and the opportunity to shape a legacy for the ones that we've lost.

First, let's start with ourselves.

As we have learned throughout this entire book, it starts with you. You need to put your own oxygen mask on before you can help others, so we are going to apply that same principle here. Let's look at our individual lives and identify how the painful experience in our life has served a purpose.

There are several ways that you are becoming a better person throughout this process. The fact that you are at the end of this book and have gone through the exercises demonstrates that you have become much more self-aware, that you have learned about boundaries and grown in your ability to establish and enforce your own boundaries in your life.

You have learned about self-care, how to be in tune with what you need, when you need it. You have learned how to be more flexible and graceful towards yourself, how to give yourself time and not be so rigid with yourself or with others. You have learned communication skills on how to vocalize to others what you need. You have learned how to put a limit on negative people and negative influences. You have become aware of the powerful effects of influences and your thoughts and you have learned how to take thoughts captive.

All of this is a result of this painful thing that happened in your life.

Clarity

Perhaps, like many others, you have experienced the gift of clarity. I do not know about you, but in the immediate days after my son's passing, life became crystal clear. I could see with a clarity that I had never experienced before. The meaning of life, along with the purpose for my life, my place in the world, and what I wanted the rest of my life to look like became completely clear.

There are people who go their entire lives, and never receive that kind of clarity.

Think back with me to when your loved one passed away and reflect on the time that has passed since then. Have you been able to gain more clarity about who you are as a person about what's important to you? Are you clearer about what you want to do professionally and what type of legacy you want to leave on this planet, or about the type of family life you want to have?

I would be willing to bet that you have experienced increased clarity in one or all those areas. That is a gift. That is a way that this event is serving a purpose in your life.

Strength

What about strength? I would bet that if we could go back in time to the month before this happened, if someone told you that it was going to happen you would have most likely said that there's no way that you would be able to survive it. You would have professed that you do not know how you could ever get through something like that.

I am guessing as well that several people have said that to you throughout this process that there is no way they would be able to get through it, or they do not know how you are getting through it.

But you ARE getting through it. And you are discovering strength that you didn't know you possessed. You found the deep reserves that only get tapped when significant adversity hits your life.

This is where the rubber meets the road.

You have discovered what you are made of and I would be willing to be it is more than you thought.

Knowing the capacity of your strength is a gift.

Having the perspective that you have faced your biggest fear in life, and that you are still standing is very empowering. The fact that you are still putting one foot in front of the other, produces a type of self-confidence that borders on invincibility. It is the perspective that you know deep down in your soul that no matter what life throws at you, you will be OK. You have the strength to handle it. That is priceless.

I have a silly example of this, but it's so true.

For all you ladies out there, we know the pain that it can be to get a bad haircut, especially for women with short hair like me. The difference between a cute, edgy, sassy haircut and looking like a 12-year-old boy is just a flick of the wrist. It is very hard to find someone who is proficient at giving a good short haircut. Well for me, since moving to Florida about a year and a half ago, I have been searching to find a good stylist.

A couple of months ago, I went to one stylist for the second time. The first time I went to her, she did a good job, so when I went back the second time, I was confident that I would get a good haircut.

Long story short, I got the worst haircut of my life. I mean, I looked like a 12-year-old Adolf Hitler! It looked like I was wearing a toupee. It was awful.

I don't mean to make light of this, but this is an actual real issue for a lot of women. A haircut like that would be enough to ruin their day, and their week; when you look in the mirror and do not like what you see, it can eat away at your security. Many women would go into hiding and wait for it to grow out before they felt they could be seen in public or have any sense of joy or self-confidence.

For me, I realized that losing your mother and son makes you able to deal with a bad haircut. I understand all things considered, that it is nowhere near the end of the world. Once you have faced a crazy mountain like this kind of adversity, all the other forms of adversity tend to fall in line for several reasons.

Number one, you are much more skilled to be able to navigate the other forms of adversity that come your way. Number two, because facing extreme adversity changes your perspective on what real adversity is.

Remember Immaculee, who survived the Rwandan genocide? SHE knows what extreme torture and mercy is, and she lived to tell about it. When she has a bad day, when it rains outside or when she's stuck in traffic, she can let it roll off her back. That is a gift the majority of the population does not possess. Most people let traffic, social media, politics and so many other things rob them of joy and laughter on a daily basis.

But we do not need to do that. We know what real adversity looks like, and we have overcome it so we can face all these other smaller forms of adversity with a lot more confidence.

Having Empathy

Another gift, or purpose for your pain that you most likely have experienced personally, is a greater capacity for empathy. Prior to experiencing loss, I tended to be a "pull yourself up by the bootstraps and charge forward" kind of person, and I found it hard, at times, to relate to people who were struggling or sad.

Now I am much more empathetic to people in their heartache.

What is fascinating to me is, I am not just more empathetic towards people who have lost a loved one, or lost a child, but I find that I am more empathetic to people in general. I have learned that adversity is relative for everyone. For every single person, the biggest challenge that you are facing or have faced, is always bigger than any challenge you have faced before. It can feel huge, daunting, and overwhelming.

I learned this lesson firsthand about a month after Quintin passed away.

I went out to dinner with some friends, and one of the couples at the table tearfully shared for 45 minutes the details of having to put their dog to sleep. Their 14-year-old dog, who was like a family member, had to be put to sleep and these people were wrecked. I mean *wrecked*. I was in awe at how devastated they were. They were barely able to hold it together at the table, having no idea what any of us at the table were walking through. They had no idea that I had just lost my son six weeks prior. I remember listening to them, and I felt real empathy for them.

My heart broke for them and the fact that they were so overwhelmed with sadness. The old Kelli would not have felt that way. The gift of empathy is being able to have a better understanding of what it is for somebody to struggle, or to better understand people who are facing grief.

That is another gift or purpose for your pain.

These are all the ways that you individually have become a better, stronger, version of yourself because of this incident.

Family

Let's talk about the impact in your immediate sphere of influence or your family. I do not know about you but losing two immediate family members has made me really appreciate and cherish the family members I do have. It has helped me to realize that time is not guaranteed

I do not know how much time I have left with the people I love in my life, whether they go first, or I go first. The losses I have had have allowed me to reveal my prioritization of those relationships, and make sure that the people I love know that I love them. I am motivated to be better and more available in their lives. I care about their hearts, and am disciplined to not get distracted by career goals, social media, or anything else that would distract me. Instead, I am intentional to invest time in and love the people that are around me.

That is a way that these losses are serving a purpose in my life.

Now truth be told, I would prefer Quintin and my mother still be here, and forego the improved relationship skills, but that is not the hand that I was dealt. It is okay to acknowledge, recognize and appreciate the fact that I am a better mother because of it. Not only do you have more awareness and clarity on the importance of your interactions and your close family relationships, but the way you are walking through this is a blessing to the people who are watching.

Whether you know it or not, you are on stage, and people around you are watching to see how you move forward from this. The way that you are tackling this, and the way that you are grabbing hold of every gift and skill set contained in this pain is speaking *volumes* to the people around you.

I can guarantee that there are cousins, aunts, or uncles that are watching from a distance and how you are handling this is teaching them that it is possible to move through and heal, and also demonstrate for them what that looks like.

When grief shows up on for them, they now have an example of someone who did it well. They do not have to wait several months and hope to have a chance meeting of an Immaculee at a conference. They have a real-life example right in front of their eyes and it is going to be much easier for them to believe that they get better and know how to do it. That is a huge purpose for your pain.

It is a huge blessing that you can be an instrument in that way for the people around you.

A Blessing to Those Around You

Let's take the concept of being a blessing a step further. What does it look like to create a legacy? How can we take this painful thing that has happened in your life and use it for significant good in the earth? Not just in your life, not just in your family's life, but for everyone.

For me, that was the founding of Qs Army. I knew right away that I wanted his death to mean something. I know every loss is significant, but you know what I mean; I wanted his death to make a difference in the world. That opportunity is available to you as well and it does not need to be anything grand in scale. It can be as simple as making yourself available to walk alongside someone else who is going through a tough time. Perhaps you decide to lead a group in your church, start a meetup group, or even just make yourself available to those that are walking through grief.

You do not need to have complete mastery. If you have seen progress in yourself, you can make yourself available to be an example to someone else. So much healing and increased learning happens when you teach someone else. I have received such a deep level of understanding and revelation as a result of writing this book; your learning always deepens when you set your mind to teach someone else.

Being an Advocate

Let's take it a step further. If the cause of your loved one's death is something that needs a voice or a champion, perhaps this is a divine opportunity for you to play a part in righting a wrong or speaking for those who cannot speak for themselves.

In Quintin's case, the issues of overdose and the opioid epidemic are huge problems in this country and need a lot of people to roll up their sleeves and commit to being part of the solution. Some of the most rewarding moments of my life have been sharing his story with people in recovery communities.

Sharing the story of his life, his death, and my heartbreak.

Each of those talks were incredibly healing for my heart, encouraging for the audience, and motivational for the people that I have been able to speak with. I have had grown men come up to me in tears, realizing the gift that is their life, and the fact that they have been reckless with it. There have been men that have come up to me in tears, expressing a sense of restoration in their relationship with their mother, understanding for the first time that their mother called the cops or kicked them out, not because she was angry or upset with them, but because she loved them and was trying to protect them. It has been so powerful.

There are so many ways to fight back and to be a part of the solution, instead of staying focused on the problem.

Moving Forward In Purpose, On Purpose

It has been so uplifting to me, writing of this book, knowing that you would be reading these words as a source of encouragement. Knowing that this book and that is going to help you find the strength, courage, and motivation to keep going. To tackle what is needed to start living the amazing life that God wants you to have.

This has become, and is, the purpose for my life. To deliver this message and to instill hope to those that need it.

Take some time now to figure out what that looks like for you.

Does it mean walking alongside someone who's stuck in grief? Does it mean becoming a part of a movement or starting your own movement?

If those do not resonate with you, just go serve someone in need. Go volunteer, go find someone that is in need, and love them well. Nothing is better for taking your eyes off your own problem than serving someone else. We all have a tendency, especially when we go through something really painful, to think that we are the only ones that are hurting, but you do not have to look very far to find someone else who is walking through significant challenges. Most likely there are people in your own community who are facing challenges bigger than what you are facing. Finding them, and serving them, is going to help you to put your own grief healing in the proper perspective.

This process is a lifelong journey and you will most likely find that it evolves over time. It is okay if you do not have to have a fixed idea about what it needs to look like.

Just know that this painful loss in your life is not in vain. It is not wasted. Your tears, your hurt, and your struggle are not for nothing.

There is an opportunity every day to use this to bless someone around you to make a difference, to make the world a better place. If you grab hold of that truth and apply it in your life, you will find that you live a very rich and rewarding life.

I would love to hear from you!

What is your framework?

How has this pain made you a better person?

What's your intention for moving forward?

What is the purpose for your pain?

I would love to encourage and support every single initiative that has been birthed out of reading this book.

I know that there are support (ahem, *Encouragement*) groups that are going to come out of this book. There are entire movements that are going to come out of this book.

And I can't wait to hear about it! Contact us at Qs Army and share your story!

Join us on Facebook or email me directly at Qsarmy@thegriefguru.com

Here's to moving forward on purpose, in purpose!

Much Love,

Kelli

Grief Assessment

Name:

Date:

Please rate each statement according to your experience today. Score each item from 0(never) up to 10(always). We will use this as a map to know where to begin and also to track progress going forward.

I have enough energy to tackle the day

0 1 2 3 4 5 6 7 8 9 10

I am getting 6-8 hours of quality, restful, sleep

0 1 2 3 4 5 6 7 8 9 10

I am able to manage overwhelming emotions

0 1 2 3 4 5 6 7 8 9 10

I am able to control and redirect my thinking as needed

0 1 2 3 4 5 6 7 8 9 10

I have a hope for a positive future

0 1 2 3 4 5 6 7 8 9 10

I feel stuck

0 1 2 3 4 5 6 7 8 9 10

I have adequate positive support in my life

0 1 2 3 4 5 6 7 8 9 10

I can see a purpose for my pain

0 1 2 3 4 5 6 7 8 9 10

I have clarity about what to eliminate and what to add in my life during this season

0 1 2 3 4 5 6 7 8 9 10

Made in the USA
Columbia, SC
20 February 2024

31842695R00100